D0572910

PARSLEY
DOUBLE CURLED

CARD SEED CO.
FREDONIA, N.Y.

CARD SEED CO.
FREDONIA, N.Y.

HERBS

CARD SEED CO.
FREDONIA, N.Y.

BEET
SWISS CHARD

LETTUCE
EARLY CURLED SIMPSON

SQUASH

CUCUMBER

ARD SEED CO.
FREDONIA, N.Y.

JAPANESE HOP

RADISH.
Long White Vienna.

SEED CO.
FREDONIA, N.Y.

HERBS
IMPROVED AMERICAN

LETTUCE

CARD SEED CO.

SMILAX

BEANS
GOLDEN WAX

ARD SEED CO.
FREDONIA, N.Y.

CARD SEED CO.
FREDONIA, N.Y.

mary emmerling's smart decorating

mary emmerling's
smart
decorating

text by Jill Kirchner Simpson   photographs by Michael Skott

Clarkson Potter/Publishers
New York

To Jimmie Cramer and Dean Johnson—and to that wonderful word—friendship!

Copyright © 1999 by Mary Emmerling
Photographs copyright © 1999 by Michael Skott

Published by Clarkson Potter/Publishers
201 East 50th Street, New York, New York 10022
Member of the Crown Publishing Group

Random House, Inc. New York, Toronto, London, Sydney, Auckland
www.randomhouse.com

CLARKSON N. POTTER, POTTER, and colophon are registered trademarks of Random House, Inc.

Printed in the United States

Design by Kayo Der Sarkissian

Library of Congress Cataloging-in-Publication Data
Emmerling, Mary.
Mary Emmerling's smart decorating / by Mary Emmerling: text by Jill Kirchner Simpson; photographs by Michael Skott. – 1st ed.
1. Interior decoration–Handbooks, manuals, etc. I. Kirchner, Jill. II. Title. III. Title: Smart decorating.
NK2115.E59   1999
747'.1–dc21   98-55418

ISBN 0-609-60325-6

10 9 8 7 6 5 4 3 2 1

First Edition

acknowledgments

I travel a lot doing photography for all my books, *Country Home* magazine (where I am creative director), and for my TV show, *Country at Home*, on HGTV. I have seen everything from the most expensive decorating ideas to the very cheapest, to even the free-for-the-taking. When the idea of *Smart Decorating* came up, I realized I was going back to my first days in New York City as an editor for *Mademoiselle* magazine. In those days, everything we did for the decorating pages was from flea markets and the streets of New York City, literally. Thursday night was when "big" trash (chairs, cabinets, trunks—great for coffee tables) was put out, and I often ended an evening dragging some great late-night find from the curb. I was hooked!

I love decorating and styling, whether it is arranging white roses in a silver vase or filling a bowl with green apples. The best part is often remembering where you found something: As I look around my rooms, I see an antique ladder from Santa Fe, old pillows from a Paris flea market, votive candles from Mexico, and necklaces from the Hamptons, and each sparks a special memory.

I can honestly say that this book, *Smart Decorating*, has been the most fun of all my seventeen books. Jimmie Cramer and Dean Johnson were the first friends I thought of to help me with it, since we have had so much fun antiquing, junking, flea marketing, shopping, and laughing at what we have found over the years. Jimmie and Dean always seem to know just what to do with a scrap of fabric, twigs, shells, children's clothes, office supplies, groceries, or odds and ends from the hardware store. Here's to twelve years of country friendship!

I am writing this during my winter vacation in the Caribbean, and even on this remote island, I have found great inexpensive decorating ideas all around me: At the restaurant last night there were big navigational maps under the glass-topped tables; in the rest room, a miniature hammock held rolls of toilet paper! So no matter where you are, you can find smart ideas. Look around your home for new ways to use the accessories you have; prowl through your favorite local stores; pore over magazines and books.

I want to thank the staff of *Country Home*, who come up with ideas every day, but especially Carol Sheehan, Jean Norman, Joe Lagani, and Frank Vitale. Thanks to Jane Perdue, Jen Kopf, Melissa Crowley, Matthew Mead, and Barbara Koppel for all their help with the Country Home Showhouse at the World Financial Center in New York, some of which is featured in this book, and thanks to Matthew for sharing even more tips. Kudos to Shelley White, Taryn Vanderford, and Elaine Walker at HGTV, who have opened so many more doors.

Special thanks, as always, to: Michael Skott, a great friend and photographer, who is always there for me and the books we do together. Gayle Benderoff and Deborah Geltman, for their never-ending support as agents. Talented friends such as Kevin Crafts, Ann Fox, Kevin Fitzpatrick, Susan Zises Green, the owners of Ruby Beets, and Liz Barbitelli, who generously shared their ideas and expertise for this book. Jill Kirchner Simpson, who is still the best writer I know. Kayo Der Sarkissian, who put photos and words together to make this book perfect. All the people at Clarkson Potter—I couldn't do any of this without them, but especially my editor, Lauren Shakely, as well as Mark McCauslin, Maggie Hinders, Joan Denman, and Catherine Sydlowski. My husband, Reg Jackson, who is the best at finding things at yard sales and flea markets and bringing them home to make me so happy. Samantha and Jonathan, who now have their own apartments and inspiration for smart decorating.

This book really makes me smile and reminds me that decorating, most of all, should be fun. I hope it does the same for you. Enjoy!

Mary Emmerling

contents

introduction

"Where do you begin when you're decorating a home?" As I crisscross the country, photographing and filming houses, it's one of the most frequent decorating questions I hear. And even if their homes are already furnished, people often assume they have to completely start over if they want to change or upgrade their look. My philosophy, however, is that where you start isn't as important as the end of the process—the finishing touches. While there is plenty of advice out there on buying furniture and coordinating fabrics, few experts focus on the details—the throws and pillows that will personalize a standard-issue sofa or revitalize a hand-me-down; the mix of candlesticks, books, and mementos that will put your individual stamp on the most basic coffee table. These small, intimate touches are what make a house a home, a place that is unique to you, and as this book will show you, they are often the least expensive elements in decorating. I never think of it as "cheap decorating"; to me it is really just "smart decorating."

While I am influenced by the architecture and location of each home I live in, I have a core "wardrobe" of furnishings that have worked for me everywhere, just like those workhorse staples in your closet that you find yourself returning to again and again. My "little black dress" of decorating includes big, comfortable white slipcovered (for practicality) sofas; wooden country classics, like a painted armoire and farmhouse table; wicker chairs and side tables that can go indoors or out and are lightweight enough to be moved; sisal carpet and a couple of kilim and Navajo rugs. The rest, as they say, is in the details:

shimmering silver candlesticks for when I want to "dress up" the house; chunky wooden ones with peeling paint when I'm feeling more down-home; vintage floral pillows when I'm yearning for old-fashioned romance; Beacon-blanket throws for rustic warmth; a leopard-print ottoman for a splash of city sophistication; santos, Mexican silver, and lots of candles when I'm in Santa Fe mode; seashells and bowls of photos and even more candles when I'm pining for the beach. Instead of redecorating my entire home, I keep the background sets the same and let the accessories become the changing cast of characters.

In any home, I think the essential elements are good-quality, comfortable upholstered furniture that can be slipcovered as your tastes and needs change; a basic complement of wooden pieces that can work in almost any setting—a dining table that can also double as a desk; an armoire that can serve as china cupboard, linen closet, or entertainment unit; smaller tables, painted benches, and trunks that can stand in as coffee tables, end tables, and extra storage; chairs that can work as easily in the bedroom as in the dining room; and a headboard or bed of your choosing with the most comfortable mattress and pillows possible (a good night's sleep is always a worthwhile investment). These basics can be family hand-me-downs, tag-sale finds, new pieces, or pedigreed antiques, depending on your inclination and budget, but I encourage you to have the patience to seek out and invest in one good piece at a time, rather than buying a house full of mediocre furniture that will need to be replaced in five years. That approach may fill rooms but is actually far more expensive and less satisfying in the long run.

I keep my walls white and my wooden floors bare, for the most part—the better to showcase a rotating shift of mirrors, prints, textiles, and accents. Window treatments and lighting should be as simple as possible as well. Like furniture, these are things that can be quite expensive to change, so keep them basic and they will work with a wide range of styles. When in doubt, choose white or black or silver.

Let the little details, which can be changed much more easily and inexpensively, set the mood. When the backgrounds are simple, a huge bucket of wildflowers gathered from a nearby field can take center stage. Votive candles can add drama for a dime, and a big basket of pinecones or pomegranates can change tune with the seasons. When curtains are simple panels looped over pegs, it's easy to change them when you happen upon a great flea market find or the summer invites a yearning for light. And when real life is the impetus for your decorating, rather than the other way around, baskets filled with everyday necessities—from paper towels to school books to sports equipment—can even become part of your decor. Paring back to the basics leaves room to find style in the everyday.

When it comes to the expense of decorating a home and the big-ticket items it entails, few of us can afford to ignore cost. And the fact of the matter is that being on a budget is nothing to be ashamed of: Having parameters helps edit the overwhelming number of choices out there, and economy often begets creativity. My most inventive friends are the ones who go junking (usually with strict self-imposed spending limits—"nothing over twenty dollars"), or who are true do-it-yourselfers and avid recyclers, or who live away from the lure of big-city stores and have to be more resourceful. They are creating the trends instead of following them, and fashioning highly personal environments that you won't find on the pages of every catalog or on the floor of every showroom.

In more than two decades of producing magazine shoots on a shoestring and decorating everything from city apartments to summer rentals on a budget, I have learned how to make almost any room look great for less money. I have had to solve the age-old decorating dilemmas—from what to place on the wall to what to hang in the windows—and have found fresh ideas to inspire you whether you live in a city loft, suburban ranch, or antique farmhouse. While all the ideas here are chosen with an eye to getting the most for your money, I think I've proven that having a budget is no reason to scrimp on style. Being savvy is what smart decorating is all about.

Shells strung on ribbon and hung at the window create just the suggestion of a curtain.

pennies

Decorating inexpensively is all a matter of perception—looking at everyday objects in a different way, finding new uses for tried-and-true elements, uncovering beauty in less expected places. It is about visiting the grocer's or the hardware store and suddenly noticing the texture in a leaf of kale or the sculptural handle of a tool. It is taking things you already have—the salad ingredients for supper, or the pennies from your pocket—and getting decorative mileage from them as well. It is changing preconceived notions—secondhand isn't necessarily second-best, and someone else's idea of trash may yield some treasures. Finding value is about seeing the subtle dignity in humbler fabrics or the artistry in a map of hairline cracks or the imprint of love in a timeworn finish. The current passion for peeling paint and rusted finishes is a perfect example—the very thing that once relegated furnishings to the trash heap now exacts a premium. Someone had to see the grace in imperfection before others followed.

from the grocer's

As my friend Jimmie Cramer once said to me, "I grow for props." While most of us grow—or buy—vegetables and fruits for eating, it never hurts to consider their aesthetic properties as well. It is hard to beat Mother Nature for color, texture, form, and variety. Green apples and lemons are tried-and-true—their simple forms and solid bright colors make an emphatic statement. But there are also less expected possibilities—scarlet runner beans, spiky fennel, fresh-laid brown eggs, and shiny black olives are worth a try. Or experiment with surprising combinations, such as mixing peppers with walnuts, onions, and pinecones. Glass jars become display cases for neat rows of preserved beans and pickles, or the translucent jewel tones of jellies (shown to advantage on a sunstruck windowsill), or herb-infused vinegars in recycled wine bottles. Simple squares of fabric or paper, tied around jar lids with twine, give a homespun appeal to jellies and preserves. Whether you have a pantry, a few open shelves, or simply a windowsill, try putting foodstuffs on display instead of hiding them away. Or liberate them from the kitchen entirely, filling a bowl, compote, or urn with fruits of the harvest on the dining room table, in the living room, or in a big basket on the front porch. While foods, with few exceptions, are always quite affordably priced, in essence they cost nothing to use as decorative accents because you still have the pleasure of eating them!

Wooden "brooding eggs," used to encourage hens to lay real eggs, are gathered in a weathered basket beside a bouquet of herbs and a bottle of rosemary vinegar.

Like sun-catchers, canning jars, **above,** containing dill and chive vinegars reflect the light as they steep on a windowsill. Their silhouetted forms become three-dimensional versions of botanical art. A fifty-cent decanter, **right,** is cleverly stoppered with a lemon instead of a cork.

In the pantry, **far left**, Shaker boxes hold foodstuffs, old glass canisters put dried herbs on display, and canning jars are resplendent with green tomatoes. Jewel-like jelly jars, **above,** are sealed with paper and twine.

Shopping Tips Seasonal Inspiration

"I always rely on the natural beauty of food," says food stylist Kevin Crafts, who prowls grocery aisles with an eye to much more than dinner. His tips for smart shopping:

• "Incredible things are now available at grocery stores and specialty stores across the United States," he points out. "Almost nothing is out of season nowadays." Fresh fruits and vegetables can make artistic centerpieces—in fact, Crafts often looks at paintings for inspiration. "I might mix three different kinds of grapes, or fresh figs and mint leaves with a white pillar candle in the center." In summer, he likes to place citrus fruits in footed bowls, then whip them up into drinks later.

• Living plants and herbs can also make great centerpieces. Crafts had a pot with three watermelon seedlings on his outdoor picnic table last summer, and just let them grow and take over the table over the course of the summer. "Purple cabbage, because it's an unusual color, also looks beautiful."

• Look for foods that come in great bottles, like olive and truffle oils, or pitted prunes in amber glass jars, which can be recycled as vases or candleholders. Passover candles in the supermarket come in clear glass votive holders for as little as a dollar.

• Don't automatically discard foods past their prime: Artichokes dry beautifully, as do many citrus fruits, so they can carry you through more than one season.

• "Whenever I'm in a foreign country, I always go to the grocery store and buy common things with different packaging—like boxes of matches, soaps, wood-handled scouring brushes—to add a little zest to everyday life."

• Like many stylists, Crafts is a believer in the beauty of candlelight. "I always use a ton of candles. I don't even have an electric fixture over my table—I have an old twisted chandelier with ten candles that lights up the room."

• Instead of expensive tablecloths and napkins, buy fabric remnants and cut and hem your own, or you can just fray the edges of a heavy linen and spray-starch it. If you don't have a sewing machine, use iron-on invisible bonding.

A stately urn filled with leeks and onions makes a handsome tableau with gardening companions of watering can and trellis. An old birdbath holds a bounty of potatoes, **opposite.**

The unexpected
combination of
vibrant orange
peppers, onions,
walnuts, and
pinecones in
a creamware
basket intrigues
the eye far more
than the standard
fruit bowl.

Humble containers, humble contents: A firkin, **far left**, cups hard-to-resist handfuls of pistachio nuts; its lid becomes the shell collector. An aquarium, **center**, makes a surprising canister for colorful dog biscuits. An old painted tin bucket, **right**, invites digging in to fresh popcorn.

A beautifully simple ironstone pedestal, originally used as a ham stand, elevates the ordinary into a centerpiece or display. A glass or ceramic cake stand can be used just as effectively. For what to place on top, almost anything goes. Try:

- **An assortment of nuts, here with garlic cloves, or other long-lived comestibles.**
- **Fresh-from-the-garden (or farmstand) produce, until it's enlisted for dinner or lunch.**
- **Stout pillar candles; this one is wreathed with sprigs of rue and santolina. Or use berries, flowers, or greens such as boxwood.**
- **Eggs: their fresh simplicity matches the style—and palette—of the pedestal.**

Keep a piece like this ironstone stand on your kitchen table, counter, dining table, or buffet to present a display that rotates by the week or even the day with fresh reminders of the season.

in flower

So often we find it hard to justify treating ourselves to fresh flowers unless company is coming or it is a special occasion. The unfortunate result is that we deprive ourselves of the companionship of flowers on an everyday basis, which is the best way to enjoy them—the soothing scent of a bedside bouquet as you awake and drift to sleep, or the cheer a cluster of bright zinnias by the sink brings to the day's daily chores. Not only should everyone try to grow or buy flowers for everyday display, but we also need to expand the definition of what is considered pretty enough to place in a vase. Greenery —whether branches from your own backyard, herbs from the farmer's market, or "filler" from the florist—is often overlooked as a thing of beauty in its own right. Ferns and wildflowers growing by the side of the road, which are sometimes even considered weeds; wheat and native grasses; humble flowers such as daisies or Queen Anne's lace; and workaday greens such as chives and leeks can all rise to the status of a bouquet, whether placed in a simple glass jelly jar or stately ceramic urn.

The container needn't be expensive or dramatic, because the flowers should take center stage. Utilitarian containers such as tomato cans (with or without their colorful labels), berry baskets (with a glass-jar liner), Mason jars, and milk bottles (along with plenty of other possibilities lurking in your recycling bin) can all be given a second life as vases. Of course, a classic vase is a

Simply green:
A small epergne
sports spiky clus-
ters of chives.

Just as pretty and more useful than flowers, a windowsill herb "garden"
keeps seasonings close at hand in the kitchen, with stems of fresh chives,
basil, oregano, and sage held in commonplace jelly jars filled with water.

good investment, and there are ample affordable examples to be found at garage sales, thrift shops, and basic housewares stores.

Just as greenery is often ignored, so too are flowers past their prime, tossed away when they could be just as easily saved and dried. Bouquets of roses and hydrangeas dry beautifully, as do bundles of lavender and many other flowering plants. The look need not be craftsy—hung by individual stems across wooden shutters or in bunches along the top of a window, dried flowers have

The romance of the rose is written across this set of worn shutters. Thumbtack individual roses or hang a bouquet upside down as their blooms start to wilt, and they will dry naturally.

No need to take a trip to the florist—just walk outside or peek into the crisper drawer. **From left:** A large kale leaf stands tall in a weathered terra-cotta crock; stone birds flock around a slender flower tin filled with drying grasses; and a large bulb of fennel sprouts unexpectedly from a bulb-forcing jar.

an artistic quality. Bundles of fresh or dried herbs can give pleasure in a vase before they add flavor to a meal.

A wonderful way to give even a few flowers greater visual impact is to use unexpected objects as flower weights in the base of a clear glass vase. A mound of pennies, cranberries, or lemon slices, a collection of buttons or shells—a surprising range of castaways make a whimsical counterpoint to the lithe, delicate stem of a flower.

Add artistry to a clear glass vase of flowers (fresh or dried) by taking liberties with the weights used to anchor the stems. Instead of the standard glass marbles or stones, try:

- **Lemon slices, whole lemons or limes, or cranberries**
- **Seashells, beach glass, river rocks**
- **Pennies, nickels, dimes**
- **Buttons, or washers and bolts**
- **Wooden or real eggs**

Anything that's weighty enough to stay under water will work. You can use flower weights to position one stem or an entire arrangement, but the visual impact is usually strongest with a single type of simple, bold flower, whether humble daisies or brilliant tulips.

natural finds

We are so conditioned to judge value by the numbers on a price tag that we often overlook the treasures right under our noses, assuming that what's widely available and free isn't worth having. Nothing could be further from the truth when it comes to nature's bounty. Pinecones and seashells, river rocks and acorns, abandoned birds' nests and bundles of twigs, whether backyard finds or mementos gathered on journeys, have a quiet, understated beauty and a resonance in the connection to the outdoors they offer us. Natural collections often look best massed in quantity in bowls or baskets, rather than left in jumbles on windowsills or dressers. Oversize sugar pinecones can fill an empty fireplace in the summer or serve as fire starters in winter; glass bowls filled with shells, starfish, coral or rocks provide a visual reminder of seaside summers even when we are miles and seasons away; rocks gathered from the top of each mountain climbed are a testament to perseverance and breathtaking vistas. Living indoors, often in cities and manicured suburbs, we are divorced from the kind of everyday relationship many of our ancestors enjoyed with the land; using elements from nature in our homes helps reestablish that link.

In addition to the expected collections, natural finds such as sticks and shells can have more functional uses. Twigs can be fashioned into clothes hangers, cutlery handles, and picture frames. Seashells attached to ribbons can serve as a natural window treatment or as tablecloth weights or candleholders. A large

Giant pinecones called sugar cones cascade over andirons to fill an off-duty fireplace with warmth.

A branch anchored in a wicker-wrapped wine bottle, **left,** becomes a whimsical photo gallery or memory board with the addition of alligator clips to hold postcards or photographs. A low bench, **below,** exhibits the serpentine shapes and mottled autumnal coloring of dried gourds.

conch shell makes a beautiful doorstop or paperweight; pinecones and clamshells form simple place card holders. Rocks and stones can serve as flower weights or rustic trivets. And there are some truly unusual (though not difficult to find) forms in nature: pebbly textured mock oranges, the Martian-like fruit produced by cousa dogwoods, the spiny shells of sea urchins, and Day-Glo-striped gourds, to name only a few. Keep your eyes open as you meander outdoors, and you are bound to discover richly tactile, beautifully sculptural finds that are free for the taking.

Genuine twigs form rustic handles for flatware. Old handles were removed, and drilled branches were glued on in their place. The rough texture of a bark vase, **left,** is the yin to a single, delicate lily's yang.

The hearth, **above,** is home to a natural tableau: Burlap is swagged across a rod made from a tree bough; abandoned birds' nests crown the mantel; and a twig basket and whisk of herbs hang by its side. At the foot of the fireplace, **right,** a basket of twigs provides ready kindling with the coziness of a nest.

Twig hangers, fashioned from sticks and curls of wire, remind us of wood's natural origins. With plain muslin dresses hung in a row on an unfinished board, they are a study in rustic simplicity.

Songs from the sea play welcome notes inside the home. Set off against a rustic basket, sea urchin shells, **above,** display their remarkable, chinalike texture. Oversize pinecones, **opposite,** exhibit a bolder texture able to fill the dark expanse of an empty hearth with broad strokes of light and shadow.

put in on paper

Among the everyday ephemera that is often simply tossed away is an abundance of paper—newspapers, books, advertisements, postcards, phone books, recipe cards, receipts, shopping bags, documents, catalogs. Especially when they are old, but even when they are new, papers have not only a graphic appeal, drawn from the rhythm of black marks against the white or yellowed surface, but also an historic interest, as a record of everyday life twenty years or a century ago. While valuable paper items—prints, color plates from old books, patterns—are usually framed, the recent trend toward pinning up papers in a more impromptu fashion is easier and less studied in its effect.

Try papering a wall with old catalog pages or printed book pages or even newspapers. Give bookshelves crisp uniformity by covering each volume in white butcher's paper or brown Kraft paper or newsprint, much like you did with schoolbooks as a child. (Books also look wonderful covered in scraps of old fabric.) Tack vintage seed packets or ledger pages to the wall of a kitchen or potting shed. Handwritten papers have a more personal character, with the strokes of someone's penmanship creating the artistry. Journal pages or hand-copied recipes offer an inside glimpse into someone else's life and have a homespun quality missing in our computer-generated age. Old labels or pictures can be affixed to jars, notebooks or boxes for a picturesque method of identification.

Traditional ephemera—advertising cards, postcards, and photographs—

Place cards for regular guests can be stashed in a serving dish, to be retrieved as needed for dinner parties, or to spark reminiscences of favorite evenings past.

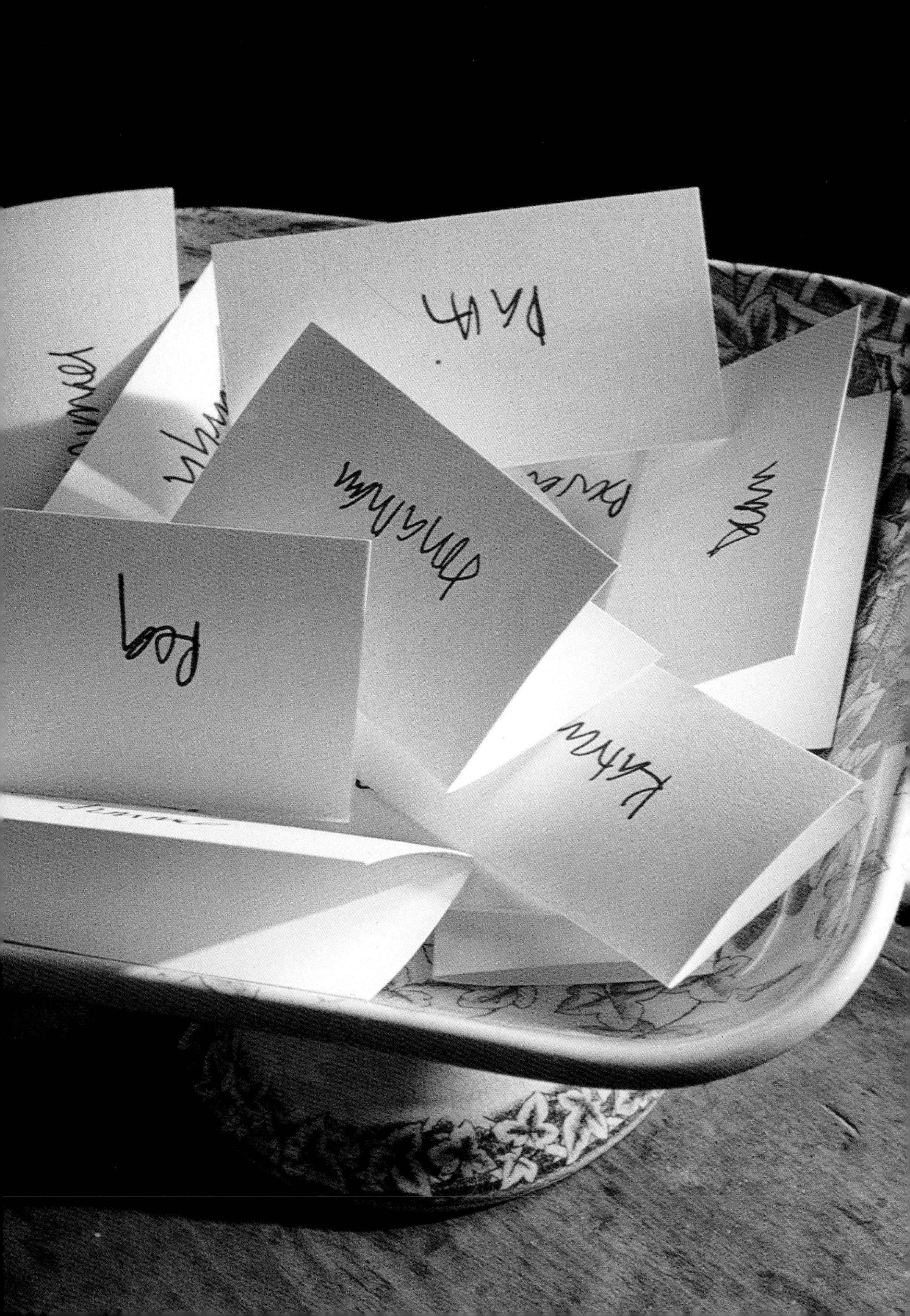

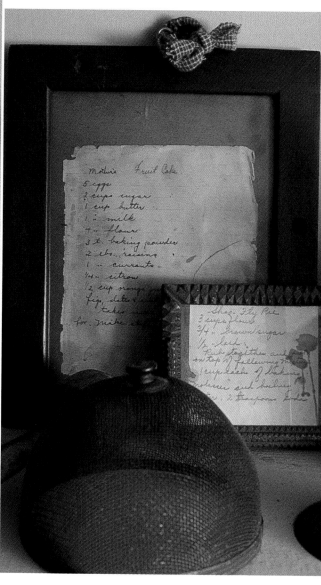

A contemporary take on ribbon-hung prints, **far left:** Black-and-white postcards are tacked onto zebra-print ribbon. Old family recipes, **center,** have been framed and ensconced in the pantry. Undistinguished books, **below,** become decorative wrapped in newsprint and homespun.

can be purchased for a reasonable price at flea markets and antiques shows, and less expected items, such as ledgers and recipes, might be found in your own attic, the recycling bin, or for next to nothing at a tag sale. Children's letters, holiday cards, vacation memorabilia, and other family mementos can be not only preserved, but displayed and enjoyed as well. And while papers don't last forever intact, even their signs of age—dog-eared corners, yellowed borders, brittle edges—can be captivating, reminding us of the bittersweet passage of time.

Brown kraft-paper book covers give disparate volumes uniformity, **far left.** Find art in unexpected places: Paper quilt templates, **above,** have been mounted on kraft paper and framed in dime-store frames painted white and crowned with recycled wire ribbon bows.

The concept of wallpaper reinvented: Old seed packets, **above**, are tacked up in a green and white medley. (Color-copy the packets to get more decorating mileage from antique originals.) Pages of newsprint affixed to the wall, **far right**, form a subtly graphic backdrop for a vintage child's dress.

Nine Lives
Finding New Uses for Old Things

Matthew Mead, a stylist and author living in New Hampshire, is a master at reinventing old pieces or creating something special out of prosaic parts. His favorite haunts include the Salvation Army, Goodwill, and state surplus stores, where outcasts from state offices and institutions often yield great metal furniture (now fetching astronomic prices at boutiques in New York's SoHo), wooden bureaus, desks and chairs, and other assorted finds. "I found some old wire rolling laundry carts that I use for potatoes and onions in the kitchen," he says. With the addition of a glass top, he points out, the wire basket would make a great coffee table. Other tips for savvy sleuthing:

• Secondhand stores are often good sources for things like old milk glass, vintage blankets, old books (cover all the volumes in the same paper for an instant library), silk flowers and ribbons (on hats or alone), and great vintage clothing—plaid Pendleton jackets, boots, straw hats—pieces Mead chooses more for their decorative potential (hung on peg racks or coat stands) than for fashion sense.

• Look for utilitarian pieces that can be creatively recycled: Mead recently took a three-tiered metal stand used in an automotive shop, lined it with moss, and created a planter.

• Keep an eye out for old lamps, which can be easily and inexpensively rewired. Often a new shade is all it takes to make a $2 lamp look like $100. Almost anything can be turned into a lamp—Mead has used everything from urns to a table leg (he used an old hat to make the shade), as well as watering cans and ceramic Art Deco vases. The Lamp Shop in Concord, New Hampshire, offers supplies for do-it-yourselfers, but many lamp shops can do the wiring for you.

• Be equally creative with the shades: Mead often uses color photocopies of things like autumn leaves, old letters and book pages, or enlargements of postage stamps or watch faces. Fabrics and linens can be adhered to styrene to form lampshades.

• Rely on color photocopies to get more miles from valuable old finds like vintage book illustrations, advertising ephemera, handwritten journals or letters, or perishable items like pressed ferns and leaves. Color copies can be framed as prints, used to découpage tabletops or boxes, or glued to the insides of cupboards and shelves. Images can even be copied onto fabric (at photo or copy shops offering T-shirt photo transfers) to create distinctive table and bed linens, throw pillows, even personalized Christmas stockings.

Old photographs
are slipped
beneath glass
to personalize
a wooden tray,
creating a
changeable
gallery of smiles.

Honest, humble, richly textured burlap epitomizes smart decorating—getting a great look for less.

dollars

Many of the objects I find attractive are old, which is a boon to decorating on the cheap. While pedigreed antiques are not inexpensive (and, in fact, increase in value), secondhand, or "already loved," items are almost always cheaper than their new counterparts. Fabric that has been used and washed and faded by the sun has a mellowed look and feel that surpasses anything brand-new. Wooden tables, cupboards, utensils, and bowls that have been worn by regular use or bruised by a child's enthusiastic play show the imprint of time and the human hand on their surface in a way that a perfect finish cannot equal. Uncovering these items may not be as simple as going to the local mall, but sifting through the jumble at a flea market, thrift shop, or relative's attic offers the thrill of finding a diamond in the rough, getting a bargain, or inventing a new incarnation for an outdated piece. Looking past or learning to appreciate imperfections and signs of age can often be a sure route to a bargain.

in the bath

Although baths are becoming more pampering, less strictly utilitarian, this is one room where the art of display is often neglected. One reason, of course, is that no one wants to ruin a fine print or the finish on a piece of furniture by exposing it to moisture. That's why decorating with inexpensive finds is especially appropriate in the bathroom.

By taking what you already own out of the medicine cabinet and putting it on display, you can change the whole feel of your bath without spending a penny. Add—if you have room—a small table, a set of wall-hung shelves, a footstool or bench, or just use the sink's vanity to create a tableau. Borrow pretty trays, cups, jars, and bowls from the dining room and kitchen to organize the essentials: Group toiletries and soaps onto silver trays or ceramic platters; decant cleansers, mouthwash, bath oils, and powders into shapely glass jars; cluster cotton balls and swabs in small bowls and mint julep cups. As with all displays, quantity elevates the utilitarian: Simple white razors look chic grouped in a bowl; an array of soaps can drip-dry atop a bed of shells, sand dollars, or river rocks instead of a standard soap dish. Gather brushes and hair-grooming supplies in one basket; cluster lipsticks and compacts in another; roll up towels and stash in a large hamper. Everything in the bath should appeal to the senses: Add small scented candles and fragrant toiletries, shimmering silver and glass, soft fluffy towels as well as textured loofahs and sponges.

A vanity can be fashioned from a simple narrow table (even a board on trestles) draped in fabric. Look beyond standard solutions: Cosmetics perch on a glass cake stand; jewelry is pinned to a satin pincushion; and heirloom photographs and silver candlesticks bestow a luxe look.

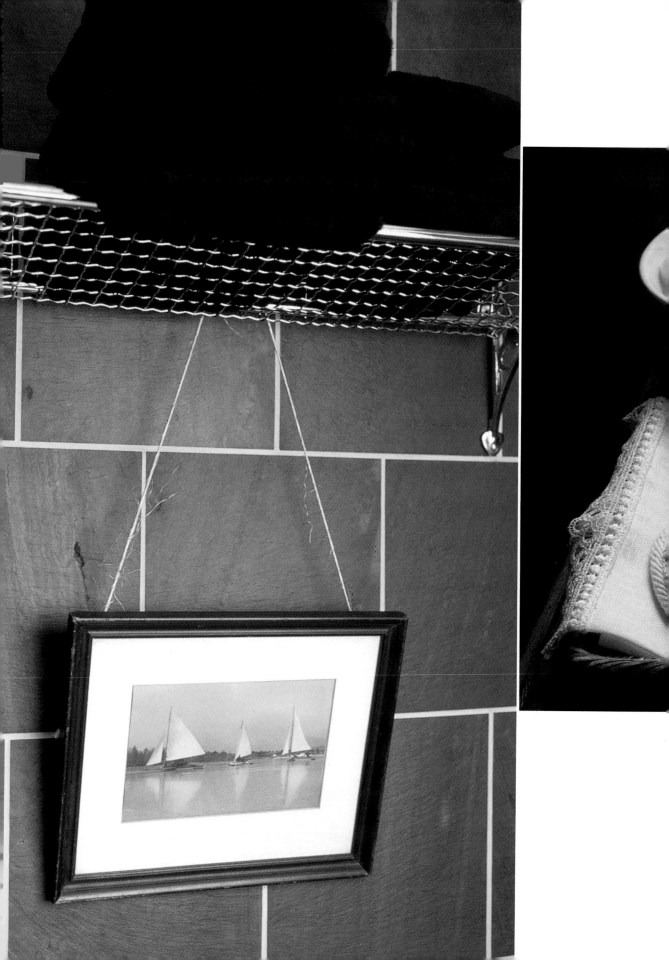

Even humble plastic razors and cotton balls can look elegant, **below,** when massed in horn and ceramic bowls and clustered on a shallow wicker tray. Art needn't be excluded from the bath, **left:** A vintage sailboat photograph, hung by twine from a chrome train-luggage rack, warms a slate-tile wall.

Introduce individuality wherever possible in a bath, because this room can so easily lapse into the routine. Fashion a shower curtain from monogrammed linens or gorgeous fabric; create a tile "quilt" on the walls using seconds, odd lots, and other bargain tiles; hang pictures on a tile wall; use a beautiful mirror instead of an institutional-looking medicine cabinet. Even the most modest bathroom can be given a distinctive personality without a costly renovation through the creative use of accessories.

Guest soaps drain on a bed of sand dollars, **left**, or line up on an antique plate, **below**. The gleam of silver, whether from a standing mirror or a mint julep cup holding toothbrush and toothpaste, adds old-fashioned glamour.

Import items from the kitchen or bar to organize the bath, **above:** A ceramic platter and glass and silver cups help give structure to clutter. Less expected than monogrammed towels, **right:** Have an oversize initial embroidered on a fabric shower curtain; fray the edge for an inexpensive finish.

Pampering pluses, **from left:** Woven slippers, wicker baskets, and a bamboo stool add texture to the sleek surfaces of a bath. Scented candles, a leopard-print jewelry roll, and reading material plump a cushioned footstool. Toiletries have poise arrayed in glass decanters and etched apothecary jars.

In a children's bath, toys and towels are gathered into a wicker basket. Odd-lot and vintage tiles (even house numbers) have been recycled to form a charming patchwork-quilt bath, **left.**

the peg-rack display

One thing I have noticed over decades of using Shaker peg racks to hold everything from coats to cameras is that whatever you put on them is elevated to the level of a display. Hung at eye level or just above, with evenly spaced pegs or hooks, peg rails serve as a kind of base on which to build a tableau. Capitalize on this quality by hanging things with sculptural shapes or a distinctive style on a peg rack: Old wire wreath forms or baskets, cowboy hats and straw boaters, bundles of dried herbs or worn painted watering cans all take on more interest hung on the wall. Clever alternatives to typical peg racks include ones made from old doorknobs or the tall spools once used for commercial sewing. Or hang a peg rack vertically—I use one that way for necklaces and jewelry. Unusual hooks or old iron nails can be lined up along a chair rail or wall to serve the same function. Peg racks have many practical applications, as well: They can stand in for a coat closet or mud room by the back door, where children can't be bothered to fuss with jackets on hangers, or line a wall in a bedroom for the same kind of easy-access storage. They can organize gear at the beach, or sports equipment by the season. Baskets, canvas bags, or fishing creels can be hung from their pegs to stow hats and mittens, cameras and film, or sunscreen and visors. But the true beauty of peg racks is that whatever you hang on them can be changed in an instant, transforming the entire room with an ever-evolving display.

A new twist on the old-fashioned peg rack: An assortment of salvaged doorknobs, from cut glass to ceramic to brass, is screwed into a weathered strip of molding to hold aprons, hats, and what-have-you.

A trio of straw hats becomes an artistic display lined up on a painted Shaker peg rail. Combining similar items draws the eye to their subtle variations.

A peg rack turned vertically provides a space-saving way to hang necklaces. Installing a length of peg railing beneath a shelf, **far left,** is an easy way to double your storage or add a picturesque display. Unexpected items like a whimsical wire chair and wooden bowls can be hung with the simple addition of wire or twine (drill a hole for hanging if necessary).

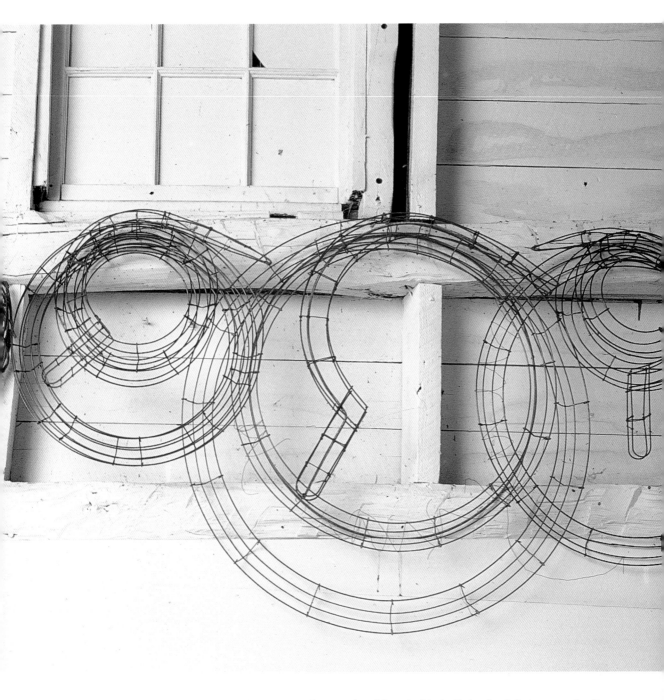

Whether an ornately carved molding studded with hooks, **left,** or a row of nails pounded into the rafters, **above,** a peg rack transforms the prosaic into the poetic. Texture comes to the fore in a lineup of straw bags and wood-handled brushes; simple wire wreath rings emphasize repetition of form.

wearable art

Choosing and hanging works of art—whether a framed painting or a quilt—seems to confound many people. The truth is that almost anything that has intrinsic beauty can adorn a wall, a door, or a set of shelves. A great example is clothing: Designed simply to cover the body and flatter the wearer, vintage clothing, from humble gingham aprons to charming baby clothes, has a surprising aesthetic appeal when liberated from the closet and put on display. Straw hats or smocked dresses can be hung on the wall; a child's first walking shoes or a pair of tiny moccasins can be showcased on shelves or cap off a stack of books. Even humble hosiery, such as old-fashioned socks in graduated sizes, can be enchanting when displayed creatively. Pillage the boxes stored in the attic to liberate christening gowns, a treasured wedding veil, your great-aunt's button-lined boots, bronzed (or plain) baby shoes, grandma-knitted sweaters, or pinafores and sailor suits from childhoods long ago. Vintage clothing, from beaded evening bags to lacy camisoles to embroidered shawls, can also be easily found at flea markets, garage sales, and thrift stores. In a child's room, you may want to consider installing a peg rack or wooden rail from which to hang family heirlooms; in a guest or master bedroom, a single padded hanger hung from a nail in the wall may host a rotating display of clothes waiting to be worn or loved but no longer in use. Favorite pieces of clothing can also be worked into a quilt or preserved in a pillow.

Shoes don't have to be bronzed to preserve them: The evanescent charm of a pair of diminutive children's moccasins is extended by keeping them on display, topping an old book or sitting on a shelf.

Bistro chairs are cleverly capped by straw hats instead of cushions. A trio of brown-and-white-checked children's aprons, **right**, creates an engaging display on the wall of a kitchen.

Old shutter panels
have simply been
propped up on a
windowsill to create
a private screen,
but they could also
easily be hinged
together and hung.

Architectural Salvage The Spirit of Invention

Ann Fox, designer and proprietor of Room Service, a store beloved in Dallas for its vintage charm and children's wares, is always finding new ways to recycle architectural salvage and add the patina of age to the new homes that are typical of Dallas. Some of her favorite style secrets:

• Use old crown moldings, pediments, transoms, even tin ceiling panels (salvaged from buildings being demolished or bought at flea markets) to add interest to walls, particularly above a bed, a sofa, or doorway, or to top a piece of art. Use old moldings and picture frames to frame a bulletin board, mirror, or to give new prints a past. Corbels make great shelf supports: four or six can create a ready-made bookcase; a pair works well for a cookbook shelf in the kitchen.

• Old glass-fronted kitchen cabinets can be turned into bookcases with just a little carpentry. Or paint or wallpaper the back panels of ready-made or built-in bookcases to give them more depth and character. "Just painting the backs one shade lighter than the wall color can add interest," says Fox.

• In an informal room lacking architectural detail, run beaded board or old barn board three-quarters of the way up the wall, then top it with a narrow running shelf for out-of-harm's-way storage and display.

• "It's relatively easy to find old kitchen tables, but what people really need are coffee tables," says Fox, "so we saw down the legs, but usually make them a little higher than the traditional coffee table."

• Use old matelassé bedspreads to make slipcovers. They've already been washed many times and preshrunk, and offer a richer look than plain white duck.

• "Just one vintage-fabric pillow in a room helps transcend the cookie-cutter look new fabrics can have," says Fox. Old samplers and needlepoint pieces also make great pillow covers. You can get more mileage from vintage fabrics and trims by using them just on the front of cushions, or pairing them with a sympathetic ticking stripe or check.

• Instead of having an uncomfortable sleep sofa, try a wicker or iron daybed plumped with pillows and throws in a guest room, child's room, office, or den. You can slip a trundle bed beneath it for twin beds in half the floor space.

• In place of hooked rugs, which have become quite expensive, look for old floral or patterned carpets that can be cut up and bound into area rugs.

• Whitewash floors in a small room to make it look bigger and more open.

cleverly contained

One way to save money (or, more important, spend it wisely) is to make the most of each thing you own. That is why I am such a big fan of baskets—I can think of a hundred different uses for them, so they never go empty or gather dust in my home. Even more utilitarian choices such as galvanized pails (from the hardware store or flower supply shop), old wooden tool or cutlery boxes, wire baskets (you can find vintage ones once used to hold gym gear in lockers, or new ones in organizer and home stores), and produce baskets (often free with your purchase at farmstands) can be put to a multitude of tasks with panache. Stylish storage options can be recycled from finds around the house: Glass jars (old spaghetti-sauce, baby-food, or other jars), terra-cotta flowerpots, or aluminum cans (with the labels removed) look great when they are lined up in quantity and filled to the brim with colorful odds and ends. For example, nail the lids of small jars to the underside of a wooden shelf and use each jar to hold nails, screws, tacks, and anchors, or paper clips, rubber bands, staples, and pushpins. (Glass jars are great organizers because they reveal their contents without being opened.) Or drill a small hole in the rim of each small terra-cotta pot, and hang them on the wall or along a piece of wood molding. Storage containers are inherently multifunctional: A rack that organizes spices in the kitchen could just as easily hold jewelry in the bedroom or baby supplies in the nursery.

The key to making visible storage look presentable is uniformity: Use one

Inside a closet, woven metal boxes and baskets organize accessories and back issues of magazines. Vintage suitcases store out-of-season clothing.

NATIONAL
GEOGRAPHIC

Lem
ON THE
ANNAPOLIS-C
RIUMPH OF
FREDERIC REMI
THE SOUTH KOR

Wire baskets offer the advantage of visibility, letting you inspect their contents instantly: A collection of old trowels is showcased in a wire basket, **left.** Oils and vinegars are corralled into a basket to reduce countertop clutter, **below,** with lemons clustered in a terra-cotta flowerpot.

kind of container, and put just one kind of item in each holder—don't mix paper clips with string and old pen caps, and don't assemble a hodgepodge of old containers on a shelf or it will look like disorganized clutter. Alternatively, choose containers that are pretty to look at in and of themselves—wicker-wrapped bottles, painted wooden boxes, vintage hatboxes, or suitcases—to hide anything neatly out of sight. Boxes, wicker hampers, and suitcases can be stacked at the foot of a bed, tucked beneath a table, piled beside a chair, or nestled atop a shelf to maximize storage space.

Counters, tables, and desktops are quickly cluttered, so if you can organize

An old wooden tool carrier makes a surprisingly useful jewelry box. Bangles are strung onto its handle; a collection of Mexican silver bracelets is gathered in tin flower cups, and necklaces spill from its sides.

A shallow berry basket puts rolls of toilet paper on display. The galvanized metal toolbox, **below left,** brings a movable feast outdoors. The well-weathered box, **bottom right,** holds candles rolled in lavender.

their contents into baskets, trays, boxes, and bowls, not only will everything be easier to find, the organizing elements themselves become a form of decoration. Sometimes I like to go for the yin-and-yang effect—for example, serving good champagne from a galvanized bucket; other times, I match the contents to the container, like paper towels in a simple wire basket. Out-in-the-open containers make retrieving and using items much easier: Keep wooden spoons and cooking utensils in a crock by the stove; stash oils and condiments in a counter-top tray where they are handy for cooking.

Many discarded (i.e., free) containers can be salvaged for home use, so keep your eyes peeled for wooden wine and produce crates, metal food tins, and

Vintage photographs are piled into a basket where they can be thumbed through and enjoyed without effort, instead of being sequestered into an album and forgotten. Wooden spoons and kitchen utensils, **right,** serve as a bouquet in a wood-slatted produce basket.

sturdy gift boxes. If you have accumulated an overabundance of canvas tote bags or interesting shopping bags, consider hanging them on the wall or a peg rack to help organize papers and projects. Pocket folders (in plain manila or bright colors) can also be tacked up on the wall to bring order to school papers, magazine clippings or household bills, instruction booklets and warranties. The drawstring fabric pouches that linens or shoes sometimes come in can hold stockings, scarves, jewelry, or mementos. Label boxes, folders, and tins attractively, with stationery-store labels or tags and neat penmanship, to add a decorative dimension to your storage.

Metal dishes organize everyday detritus into a tableau: Spare change, playing cards, and pinecones become curious, but effective, tablemates. A silver frame and loving cup complete the picture.

Spices bought in bulk, **above,** should be decanted into airtight glass canisters like these metal-lidded apothecary jars. Fabric-lined baskets, **left,** once used for rising bread dough, are a natural choice for putting ingredients within easy reach in the kitchen. Shallow baskets are also smart for keeping rolling pins and paper towels in place.

Because of their deep, ample size, the galvanized metal buckets used by florists to hold their wares are surprisingly handy around the house. In addition to using them for cut flowers (few vases give as much support for long stems), try using them to stow:

- **Paper towels, wrapping paper, foil, and plastic wrap**
- **Fresh herbs or plants, either in cut bundles or planted in the bucket**
- **Champagne or wine or ice**
- **Potatoes, onions, apples, and other produce**

Look for sturdy, well-made buckets at floral supply stores and in garden catalogs. Enamel-coated metal ones are also available, for a slightly more polished look. The best-made (and most expensive) buckets are French, but anything with strong, watertight seams will do.

fabric fixes

Fabrics are a wonderful camouflage for cheap finds that are old, worn, or in states of minor disrepair. Fabric-covered cushions can soften a hard wood or fraying woven seat; pillows can brighten a nondescript sofa or strategically cover spots on a club chair; a throw can serve as a loose slipcover. You might find a table for a great price because it needs refinishing—just drape a table-cloth or swath of fabric across it. Many people avoid using fabric simply because they are not confident sewers, but there are many quick and easy short-cuts that require little or no stitching: Vintage cushion covers, pillow shams, tablecloths, curtains, and table runners can often be used as is. Clip-on curtain rings can be added to dresser scarves, pillow slips, or runners to create instant café curtains. Use a piece of cording to secure a piece of fabric as a "slipcover" over a chair seat. Tie knots in each corner of a scarf and use it as a seat cover or to line a basket. Mosquito netting or a sheer fabric can be tacked with pushpins to create an impromptu canopy above a bed. Sturdy fabrics such as burlap can be stapled over walls in poor condition. And if you need to shorten or hem a piece of fabric, try using iron-on fusing instead of sewing.

Whether you buy new or secondhand, it pays to stick with simpler fabrics, especially when you need a lot of yardage. Utilitarian choices such as muslin, canvas, mattress ticking, denim, homespun, burlap, and cheesecloth are well priced and well suited to simple country interiors. Shop for remnants and

A swath of basic burlap becomes an impromptu awning knotted and slung across a trellis.

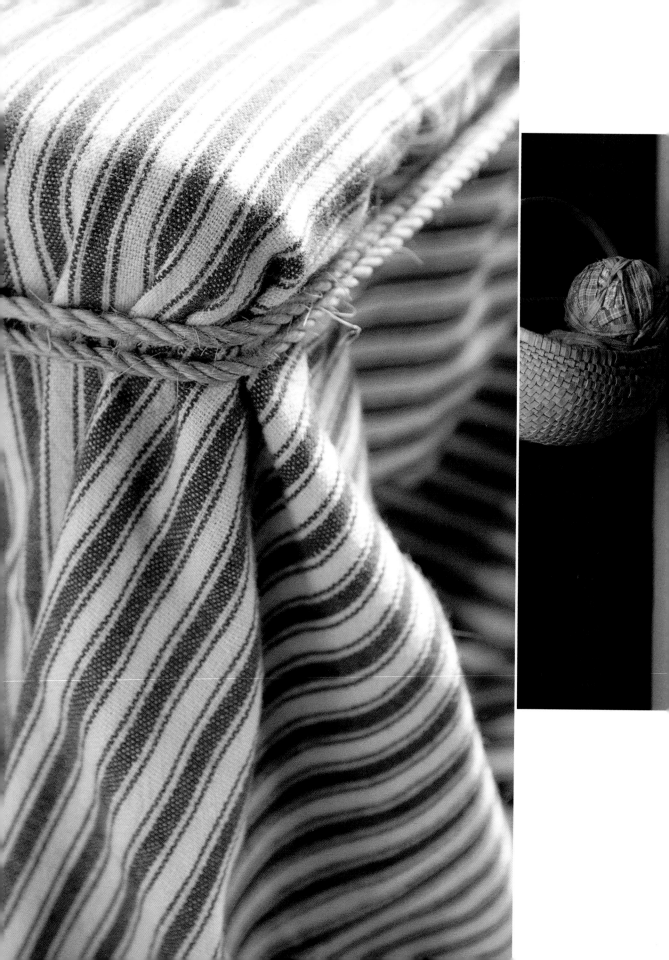

Far left: Rope secures a square of ticking-stripe fabric for quick camouflage of a stool. Vintage feed sacks, **center,** have been nailed to the wall for unorthodox storage and intriguing display. Sheets of linen homespun, **below,** are showcased on a blanket rack; they could also be draped over a railing.

manufacturer's seconds; check out theatrical suppliers for inexpensive scrim, velvet, and other fabrics by the bolt.

Fabrics can be easily recycled as well: The curtains your sister has tired of might make a great tablecloth or duvet cover for you; your grandmother's lace tablecloths could be reinvented as light-filtering curtains; almost any remnant (even clothing) can be reincarnated as throw pillows. Other than paint, few things offer as many possibilities for change as fabric.

Stockings are hung on a peg rail with care, in an enchanting lineup of graduated sizes. Home-spun fabrics are stacked on the shelf above; rush mats hung beneath add interesting texture (and could camouflage a bad wall).

Cushions and covers can help salvage seats past their prime. A flat cushion, **this page,** is draped over a stool; loops of buttons weight its corners to keep it in place. A plain damask slip-cover, **opposite,** skirts the seat of this painted wooden chair.

cutting costs on fabric

While fabric can make a room, it can also quickly break a budget, especially when large quantities are involved. Kevin Fitzpatrick, head of City Workroom in New York, offers this advice:

• Watch out not only for the cost per yard, but also for the size of the repeat within the pattern. A large pattern can add ten yards to a drapery order.

• Stay with solids, stripes, neutrals, and basics in lower-priced fabrics; reserve higher-end fabrics, which are better for color and pattern, for small pieces like pillows, throws, or an ottoman, which will still have a strong impact.

• Check out "mill end" outlets or factory stores for great bargains on discontinued fabrics, overruns, or fabrics with slight imperfections.

• Economize on trims, which can also increase costs exponentially. For a crisp finish on curtain headings or borders, topstitch inexpensive grosgrain ribbon instead of a pricey fringe. Or unravel the edge of a woven fabric to create a fringed effect.

• Look for old draperies and fabrics at tag sales and flea markets. "I bought a thirty-year-old Schumacher hand-loomed silk damask that would have cost six hundred dollars a yard for about ten dollars a yard at an antiques show," says Fitzpatrick. He advises relining old draperies with new fabric and airing out vintage fabrics on the clothesline rather than dry-cleaning them. To lengthen draperies that are too short, add a border of contrasting fabric with mitered corners on the bottom and sides.

• You can often color-correct spots on old fabric with crayons or markers—if your curtains are full no one is likely to notice.

• If the style of the room is masculine, don't overlook good-quality men's suiting shops. Flannels and wools are often much less expensive there than they would be at a home furnishings store.

• Similarly, lower-priced dress fabrics, such as cotton prints and ginghams, work well for kitchen curtains. The yardage is narrower, but often so are kitchen windows.

• Old silk scarves make wonderful pillow faces. Fitzpatrick once upholstered an old Hermes scarf on top of an ottoman.

• Provide your own drapery lining rather than having the workroom supply it, and shop for it on sale. Also, shop labor prices for fabrication: They vary widely.

• Keep the style of your curtains simple. Fortunately, simple is the trend of our times. Anything nonstandard or detailed—piping, mitering, or self-ties—will cost more.

Old linen sheets
have been sewn
into pillows, then
decorated with
evocative flower
names—"Calla
Lily," "Clematis"—
written in fabric
marker.

A piece of vintage fabric is draped over two hooks to form a window swag (a good strategy when you don't have much yardage). A softly sheened stripe of monogrammed damask, **opposite**, contrasts with the rougher textured tablecloth layered beneath it.

Old lace tablecloths lose their fussiness but not their charm when draped over casual furniture outdoors.

can this fabric be saved?

Many fabrics and linens at flea markets and estate sales are in less-than-perfect condition, and it is sometimes hard to evaluate whether a piece can be repaired or cleaned. Liz Barbitelli, owner of The Laundry at Linens Limited in Milwaukee, Wisconsin, offers these pointers:

• Carefully inspect any item you are considering purchasing. Even a folded piece can be unfolded section by section without completely spreading it out. If someone balks at showing you the fabric, there's probably a reason.

• If fabrics are yellowed or grayed from age, laundering can probably restore them to their original color. It can be hard to repair moth holes, tears, and other damage requiring mending. Instead, consider using the undamaged part of the cloth for a pillow top or small café curtain, or patching it with a pretty fabric.

• To remove stains on washable fabrics, Barbitelli advises soaking the item overnight in lukewarm water with mild detergent. Plain detergent is best; additives, brighteners, and whiteners can fade colors. Rub a little on spots, and then let soak.

• Put linens, especially if they have cutwork or embroidery, into a fully loaded washing machine (you can add sheets or towels) with water set at warm. Treat spots again if necessary by dabbing them with a bit of full-strength bleach on a Q-Tip, rather than bleaching the whole item. Rinse well.

• Always line-dry linens and delicate fabrics: Heat, whether from the washer, dryer, or iron, contributes to wear and tear.

• To protect cutwork and embroidery, iron the piece, wrong side up, on a towel.

• To remove candle wax from a tablecloth, run the spot under very hot water, or lift it by placing a double thickness of paper towels over the spot and running a warm iron over it. Don't scrape the cloth with a knife, as that could damage the fibers. Flush grease spots with hot water as well, then soak in mild soap and water. Wine spots should be soaked in cold water, and ink, unfortunately, is virtually impossible to remove. "Not every stain comes out," warns Barbitelli. "But that doesn't mean a piece isn't usable—most of the time you won't even notice stains when a tablecloth is in use. And if you're not using your linens, what's the point in having them?"

• Consult a professional for cleaning heirloom or valuable linens or intractable stains. A laundry or seamstress specializing in restoring old linens, such as Linens Limited, can often remove stains and make repairs, even matching old embroidery.

Inexpensive mosquito netting hung by alligator clips and cord thumbtacked to the ceiling becomes a romantic canopy. An old garden trellis and flat columns form a stately "headboard."

illuminating ideas

Candles are in every thrifty decorator's bag of tricks: Nothing else can conjure up mood, atmosphere, and romance so easily and inexpensively. From stout pillars to diminutive votives, candles are widely available and affordable enough to use in quantity, which is what gives the greatest impact. Because candles are so ubiquitous, however, it's worth going an extra step to give them distinctive style. Holders fashioned from unexpected objects, though quite utilitarian in themselves, make for wonderfully intriguing candlesticks. Tiny tart pans affixed to the heads of old shovels and rakes create whimsical sconces, while old graters, simply placed over votives, cast a magical glow. Tapers can be anchored in sand inside dime-store drinking glasses or galvanized pails or lodged in bud vases or bottles. Votives can be lined up on a collection of miniature chairs or tucked inside jelly jars. Be on the lookout for orphans that can be rescued by candlelight: Electric sconces and chandeliers that no longer work can be fitted with candles instead; a lantern that's lost its post or glass can still hold a candle. Branches make clever garden stakes affixed with votive holders for outdoor lighting. A cluster of candles can be casually held in a watering can; pillars can be grouped on a cake stand. Just remember that a candle flame can start a fire; ensure that your makeshift candleholder is heat resistant and never left unattended while the candle is lit.

Inexpensive sources for candles and holders include dime stores, church

Clever, cheap, and easy, these old graters are an unexpected variation on pierced tin votive holders, casting a magical glow through their pores.

Glass reflects light, making it an ideal candleholder. Glasses inscribed with religious sayings (or almost any small drinking glasses) make natural votive holders. The inexpensive jelly-jar glasses, **right**, are filled with sand to anchor tall tapers.

candles, floral and restaurant supply stores. Buy votive candles by the dozen and use them to line mantels, windowsills, and doorframes for romantic ambiance during a party, or place them along porch railings and walkways to help guide people's way in the evening. Pillars of varying sizes can be grouped together to striking effect; place them on a platter or a bed of cabbage leaves or foliage. Hollowed-out fruits and vegetables such as apples, limes, artichokes or squash can make clever cut-rate candleholders as well. Use the season and the setting—or pure imagination—to inspire fresh ways to enjoy the timeless beauty of candlelight.

Shapely colored-glass bud vases, **left,** another dime-store find, easily accommodate tapers in their slender grasp. A galvanized watering can, **right,** casually holds a whole cluster of candles (be sure they are arranged securely before lighting).

Inventive adaptations, **from left:** An old garden-stake torch, minus its hurricane glass, now stands guard beside a fireplace. Utilitarian shovel and rake heads become whimsical wall sconces with the addition of tiny tart pans soldered to their stems to hold votive or taper candles.

Unusual spiral-shaped candles animate a collection of stately silver candlesticks. While basic white is always right, candles in distinctive colors or shapes, or even broad stripes, can add an extra spark. A simple wrought-iron candle chandelier, **right,** is bedecked in a magnificent array of beaded garlands and necklaces.

at your service

One of the best bargain decorations for your walls isn't found in a frame, but inside your kitchen or dining room cupboards: Hanging an arrangement of old (or new) plates and platters on the wall is a traditional display idea enjoying a comeback, as people branch out from matched sets and experiment with using all-white plates in modern settings, or grouping flea market finds by color or style. In fact, the best way to find old china for a song is not to look for perfectly matched sets: Transferware plates with a few chips or cracks, beautiful china orphans that have lost their brothers and sisters, oversize platters that can't be easily accommodated in cabinets, or even the simple lids to ironstone tureens and serving dishes (which would be quite expensive if paired with their bottoms) become artful elements hung on the wall. Group items together by shared colors or shapes—all ironstone saucers or blue-and-white patterns, for example—and hang them with plate hangers or prop them on ledges or shelves (use plate stands or push pins to hold them in place). Platters, trays, and plates can then be taken down as needed for serving, for the bonus of space-saving storage. Don't overlook hand-me-downs from your grandmother, camp ceramic projects crafted by your children when they were young, or the wedding china serving pieces you never seem to use. Even broken crockery, whether excavated at yard sales or salvaged from household accidents, can make a miniature archaeological tableau arranged in a dish or on a wall or table.

Old, imperfect creamy ironstone plates and a brown-and-white transferware platter make a pleasing display on the wall and can be taken down for serving as needed.

Strategies for affordable collecting: The lids to ironstone and china soup tureens are much less expensive than the tureens themselves; orphaned plates are less dear than those in matched sets. Display lids on the wall, **far left,** or stack platters in a plate rack for easy access, **above.**

Even in a potting shed or pantry, grace notes are appreciated. An old painted tole tray, peeling and rusted, is no longer practical for serving, but it still lends a decorative fillip propped upon a weathered beam.

The door of an 1820s Tennessee corner cupboard is left ajar to display a collection of creamware and transferware plates in daily use, **above**. An alphabet plate is placed atop an old quilt pattern and, with a miniature wheelbarrow and twig pencils, forms a rustically hued tableau, **left**.

affordable art

Art, because it is perceived to be so costly, is often one of the most intimidating decorating purchases, usually because "art" is so narrowly defined. One of the glories of American country style is its appreciation for seeing artistry in the everyday. When I first began collecting, I hung antique checkerboards, cutting boards, and quilts on my walls because I couldn't afford traditional "art." My huge American flag still hangs in every home I live in, and a beautiful empty frame usually pleases me more than a precious painting on my wall. Taking a less reverential approach to art offers more flexibility in your decorating scheme—you don't have to design a room around a masterpiece—and is certainly more wallet-friendly. Almost anything is elevated to art when you place it in a frame: Quilt patterns have the fluid geometry of Matisse cutouts; hand-pressed flowers and ferns eclipse cookie-cutter Redouté prints. Pieces of embroidery or old fabric, vintage menus or magazine covers, souvenirs and scrapbook pages—there is an unending wealth of raw material for framing. As with other decorating elements, framed pictures—especially small ones—have much greater impact in multiples. One old-time class photo is a curiosity; a wall covered in them becomes compelling. Consider art in the making: a changing rotation of children's pictures tacked to the wall (on a piece of molding or a large bulletin board), or an oversize blackboard or slates on the wall where each member of the family can be their own Picasso.

A bulletin board is a work in progress, a collage of daily jetsam, inspiring images, and meaningful mementos.

RUSTIC STAND OF FLOWERS.

BOUQ

A trio of botanical prints, in a range of styles, is united by naturally
finished wood frames to lend grace to a bath. Money-saving alternatives
include calendar pages and color-photocopied prints or book plates.

OF FLOWERS.

PICK UP

FLOWERS
MILK
BREAD
CRAB CAKES

A large piece of metal once used for fire protection behind a wood stove has been recast as a chalkboard—for grocery lists or family communiqués. Black-and-white photographs, **right,** framed in wide mats and simple black frames, give a room a modern frisson.

Old American flags, an Emmerling favorite that blends easily into any decor, have been framed in sympathetic peeling white wooden molding.

This often overlooked but necessary accessory can go far beyond the ugly rubber wedges sold at the hardware store. In addition to the figurative iron doorstops that are available, there are many more inventive possibilities you might find about the house or garden. Consider:

- **A garden urn, in this case capped by a large ball of twine**
- **A footstool or small bench**
- **A pumpkin, real or faux**
- **A nest of terra-cotta pots, weighted with a heavy stone if necessary**

A stack of books, a piece of statuary, a coin-filled piggy bank, or a large stone are other potential candidates. Whatever the doorstop, it need only be heavy enough to hold a door open in the breeze, light enough to move as needed, and not so bulky as to obstruct traffic.

frames for a song

These days, the frame is likely to cost even more than what is inside it: Antique, intricately carved, gilded, or well-crafted frames can be shockingly expensive. At the same time, good, basic ready-made frames are being offered at art supply and housewares stores at very reasonable prices, and can be given a custom look for less money with hand-cut mats (the paper or fabric-covered frame within the frame). I also find good bargains to be had at tag sales and flea markets, where many people might pass up an unattractive picture but not notice its frame, a Cinderella in waiting. Old frames can often be cut down by a framer to the size you need, and loose joints repaired. A framer may also be able to fit a beautiful frame with a mirror (have it cut to size by a glass cutter). You may want to consider painting a gaudily ornate frame white or a simple frame with a damaged finish black. I also love to fit an attractive frame with cork to make a more sophisticated bulletin board for a home office or workspace. Or leave beautifully aged frames empty, and let the frame be the decoration. Inexpensive picture frames can be dressed up in a multitude of ways—try covering them with colorful postage stamps, old buttons, millinery flowers, seashells or tiny pinecones, gold ornaments from a crafts store, vintage bottle caps, colorful dime-store charms, mementos from a trip, or copper pennies. Another popular frame conversion is to fit an old window or doorframe with mirrors or inexpensive prints in place of glass panes.

An engaging collection of hand-crafted items in a rustic brown palette, from miniature log cabins to stuffed fabric birds to button samplers, adorns the wall of this workshop.

My philosophy has always been that it is the little things that make a difference. So when it comes to the big pieces, I believe in investing in straightforward, good-quality furnishings. They may not be cheap (unless you happen onto great secondhand finds), but will end up being a bargain in the long run, because they will never go out of style and you can use them absolutely anywhere, whether it's down sofas slipcovered in basic white or painted cupboards and armoires. What adds personality are all the smaller touches I like to focus on: the tableau of accessories on a tabletop or filling a bookshelf; the baskets that organize the necessary clutter of everyday life; the pictures and peg racks that warm a wall. When it's time to look for high-ticket items, simplicity is paramount: canvas covers on the sofa instead of a print you'll tire of, humble farmhouse tables instead of fresh-from-the factory dining furniture. Don't downgrade your approach according to the price tag; almost anything can look beautiful with just a little care.

savvy storage

The true storage problems are not always what we—or the organizing experts
—expect them to be: The solutions are not always as simple as adding more
shoe racks in the closet or CD racks in the den. Recycling, now practiced in a
majority of communities, has presented a whole new set of storage (and sorting)
challenges. Pets require a surprising amount of gear, not to mention bulky
comestibles. Gift wrapping, if you love it, can quickly commandeer a chest or
closet. Magazines and catalogs proliferate; cameras and film can't be found
when we need them. Most of us require a home office even if we don't hold a
regular job, and laundry areas are seldom as nice as we would like them to be.
Meeting these needs doesn't require much room, just a corner or small stretch
of wall or floor—probably the same amount of space the clutter takes up any-
way, but organized so that it makes the task of feeding the cat, dressing up a
package, or ordering from a catalog efficient and fun.

A wrapping center has long been a fantasy of mine and many people I know.
One can be easily fashioned from dowels suspended between two vertical peg
racks to hold numerous rolls of paper and ribbons, so wrapping becomes less of
a chore or hunt for stray materials and more of a creative, enjoyable endeavor.

Dog gear can be organized in an unused corner with peg racks to hold leashes
and collars; small freestanding shelves for food and treats; bowls for bones and
play toys; and a basket of towels for drying off a wet pup. Make a laundry area

A stack of vintage
suitcases at
the foot of the
bed, along with
a galvanized
metal bin, forms
a blanket chest of
sorts, holding
bedding and out-
of-season clothes.

Boxes covered in elegant, old wallpaper are tagged with their contents, from gift wrap to Christmas decorations. A window box with a miniature trellis, **far right,** makes a picturesque desk organizer; a corkboard looks posh in a carved picture frame.

more inviting with a tailored skirt for the laundry sink, a table for folding clothes, and attractive shelves for laundry supplies. Instead of plastic bins, outfit a recycling area with wicker baskets and big, chunky balls of twine and scissors for easy tie-ups. Keep entertaining supplies at the ready on a bar cart or side table set up with bottles of wine, liquor, and mixers; tumblers, shot glasses, and wineglasses; cocktail napkins and hand towels; ice bucket, cocktail shaker and strainer, bottle openers and corkscrews.

We all need an area in which to file important papers, pay bills, write letters, and generally keep track of our lives. Setting up a desk devoted to the purpose, with good filing drawers; plenty of folders, stationery, and stamps; and possibly a computer, makes all those dreaded chores much easier to achieve. Carve

Baskets can help tuck storage into the least likely of spaces: Here, nestled beneath the eaves on a high shelf, a collection of vintage baskets in every shade of green does more than look pretty—stowed inside are such modern-day necessities as bank statements, CDs, and office supplies.

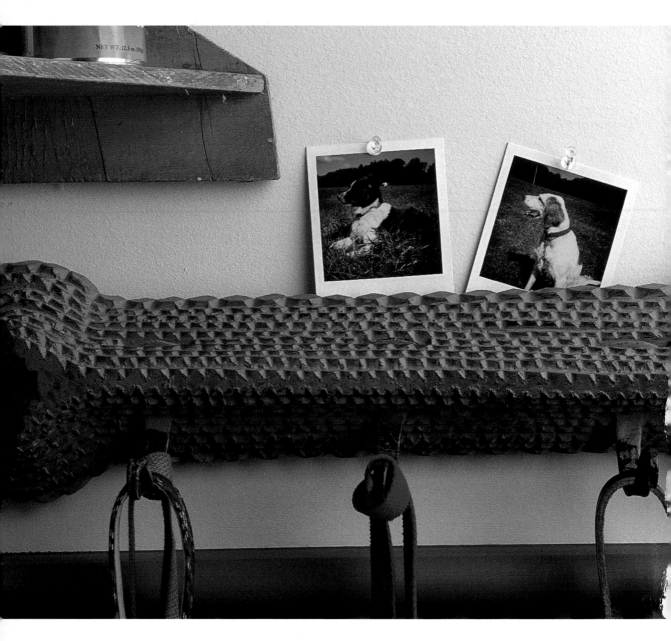

out space in an alcove or hallway, a corner of your bedroom, kitchen, or den, or devote an attic room to an office hideaway. Instead of unattractive metal filing cabinets, consider using file baskets, or create a skirted fabric cover for a table and hide files and supplies underneath.

Always be on the lookout for large, deep baskets, whether wicker or wire, which can hold everything from mail and magazines (clip out just the articles or photos you're interested in to save space) to camera and sporting equipment, hats and mittens, CDs and videos. You can find them at discount and import stores, flea markets, and tag sales, and they will never go out of style.

Fido is organized in fine fashion with a bone-shaped tramp-art peg rack holding leashes and collars, **above,** with cameo photos tucked in the top. Rawhide "bones" (in a bowl for easy access) and toys are stored on a matching bench, **right.**

A glass filled with wooden-handled brushes helps keep a kitchen sink organized. A laundry sink, **left,** transcends the utilitarian and provides extra storage with a crisp striped skirt; it's also a good spot for arranging cut flowers.

Two peg racks, hung vertically, support dowels that hold rolls of wrapping paper and ribbon. A peg rack underneath keeps scissors handy.

Auctions, Estate Sales, Tag Sales, and Flea Markets
Shopping Smart

It's all rather hit or miss, but once you get to know the options in your area, you'll develop a feel for where to look for the best deals:

• Auctions, particularly in the country, but also at second-tier auction houses in large cities, can provide the best bargain hunting. Go ahead of time to inspect the merchandise, if possible, and fix a price limit in your mind so you don't get carried away in the heat of a bidding war. Storage and moving companies often have periodic auctions to unload unclaimed merchandise; while these are extremely uneven (you sometimes can't even see what you're bidding on), great bargains can be had. Bank foreclosures can also lead to furniture auctions; check your newspaper classified section for notices.

• Flea markets and swap meets vary in quality, but in general they offer the greatest quantity of authentically old merchandise to peruse. You'll pay for the editing a dealer has done for you: no rock-bottom prices, but still less than most antiques stores, and you can always bargain. Check your local newspaper or antiques papers, such as *Antiques & The Arts Weekly* or *Maine Antiques Digest*, for listings.

• Estate sales are usually (but not always) run by professional firms to sell the entire contents of a house after someone's death. While the prices aren't a steal, the goods are usually of better quality (and quantity) than a tag sale.

• Garage sales, tag sales, and yard sales are usually held by individual homeowners, or sometimes a group of neighbors. These require the patience to check out dozens of possible candidates before you're likely to find anything you love, but the potential for uncovering an amazing deal is motivation enough for many to make the Saturday morning pilgrimage (serious sales are often held on Fridays as well). Look for ads that list "furniture" instead of just "bric-a-brac" or "children's clothes." Unfortunately, eight times out of ten, you'll find a homeowner who has overvalued, rather than undervalued, their possessions.

• Also, don't overlook church sales, thrift shops, and secondhand furniture stores, which don't put on the airs of antiques shops, and don't jack up their prices as high, either.

multiple choice dressing up a cupboard

Even a simple shelf looks more interesting with molding or a pediment applied to the surface, or with a dramatic display of intriguing objects. Antique odds and ends create a changing landscape atop this white painted cupboard:

- **A pair of tin finials flank a ball of string nestled in a bowl.**
- **A concrete garden ornament adds a distinctive flourish.**
- **Framed white-on-white quilt squares and elegant embroidery bring delicacy.**
- **A collection of green- and whitewashed wooden finials lends an architectural air.**

Look around your house for urns and vases with interesting profiles, architectural fragments, collections, or works of art to add detail to cupboards, bookshelves, and flea-market finds. Symmetrical arrangements give the effect of greater formality, while random displays suggest a more casual ease.

windows of opportunity

Window treatments, particularly when they involve reams of fabric and lining and interlining, can be a surprisingly expensive component of decorating.
But luckily, lighter, less formal curtains (which are also significantly less
costly), have come into fashion, liberating windows and letting in the sun.
Most window treatments must be custom-made to fit each window, which
increases the expense exponentially, but there are more good ready-made
options than ever, and easy ways to add custom details for very little money.

For a vintage look, consider adapting old curtains to your windows, or
adding period trim to new panels. Beacon blankets, quilt tops, matelassé bedspreads, and damask tablecloths can all make wonderful one-of-a-kind curtains
as well. A shawl can become a cozy valance, and a simple lace dresser scarf or
pillow sham could serve as a café curtain, clipped to a rod. Another easy option
is to dress up ready-made panels of linen, muslin, cotton, or canvas with grosgrain ribbon or trim along the leading edges and hems, or to use ribbon ties in
place of (or in addition to) curtain rings. Simple panels could also be edged or
lined in a contrasting print, check, or stripe for extra richness. Sew a row of old
buttons, shells, or *milagros* or charms to a curtain, or use a cluster of vintage
millinery flowers as a tieback.

The way you hang curtains can also add a distinctive layer of detail: A fresh
approach is to sew small loops to the top of a curtain panel, and then hang them

Shells culled from walks on the beach have been drilled with small holes and wired onto the hem of a sheer curtain, weighting it in the breeze and adding seaside charm to a plain ready-made panel.

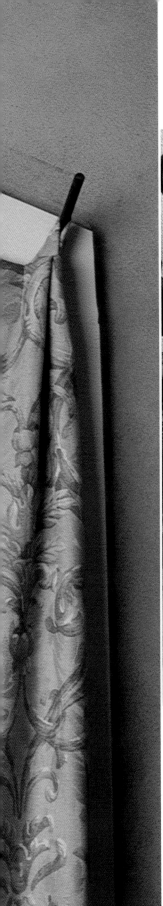

The curtain, **left,** was sewn with pleated loops designed to hang on pegs. A wool shawl serves as an informal valance. The crisp toile, **below,** is edged in grosgrain ribbon, with alternating black and white bows attached to the rings. Each panel is hung from a separate, overlapping iron rod.

by pegs or hooks above the window. This offers the flexibility of folding the curtain back for light and views or leaving it closed. Or hang two curtain rods instead of one (if they're delicate enough), placing one panel on each rod. Even if you can't sew a stitch, a long swath of sheer fabric can be swagged across the top of a window and down the sides for an enchanting effect. Don't worry too much about curtain length—curtain hemlines are not as sensitive to the whims of fashion as are women's dresses. If a panel is too short, and trim doesn't extend

A dresser scarf, linen hand towel, or pillowcase can form a pretty café curtain. Seek out old linens embroidered with your own initials.

it sufficiently, a panel in a contrasting color but similar fabric can close the gap. If a velvet drapery from mail order is a few inches too long, let it "puddle" on the floor for a nonchalantly elegant look.

Wooden blinds, bamboo and tortoise-look blinds, and Roman shades are other, more tailored options. Shutters can be expensive, but old ones are widely available at flea markets—you may be able to find ones that will fit your windows well enough to fit the bill.

Wooden pegs, metal hooks, or small knobs can be installed above a window for minimalist curtain hanging. The simple checked-weave panel, **left,** can be hung by one or more fabric loops depending on the privacy desired. **Below,** the same curtain is ornamented with milagros (small tin religious figures) and silver charms.

Filmy gauze suggests just the ghost of a curtain, casually knotted instead of drawn. A sheer gathered panel on an interior door, **opposite**, softens the transition between public and private space.

Color and Texture Making Cheap Look Chic

Designer Susan Zises Green works for a high-end clientele in New York and Nantucket, but many of her decorating ideas are refreshingly down-to-earth. Her recommendations for budget-conscious design:

• "Cover walls with a simple cotton, burlap, or felt. You can have felt paperbacked and applied to the walls like fabric. Or cover walls with kraft paper (the kind used for wrapping packages), which turns a rich, velvety brown when varnished. It can be cut up into squares and applied so you can see the seams, with just a hint of color peeking through (paint the walls clay, brown, or gray).

• Paint floors if you can't afford to have them refinished. You can also paint or stencil a sisal rug. Or buy small, inexpensive rag rugs and sew them together. When in doubt, says Green, choose sisal: "It's still a wonderful choice and very affordable." Another good source for rugs: tag sales.

• "Plain muslin makes a beautiful curtain," says Green, who's been known to use this affordable fabric even on high-end jobs. "You can add a border or ribbon, or even paint it with acrylic paint." Or paint plain roller shades, which was often done in the 1930s; look for old dark green schoolhouse shades, and add gold stars or cranberry stripes. Theatrical gauze or scrim, edged in cotton binding, and terry cloth are other favorites of Green's. Her rule of thumb: "If unlined, curtains should be very full."

• Use rubber stamps (there are now larger-scale ones designed for decorating projects) to add a simple design, such as stars or a scroll border, to walls or curtains.

• In addition to tag sales, look in the classified ads under "Merchandise" for people selling furniture when they are moving; check out foreclosure sales, church sales, and even the dump, which in Nantucket is known as the "Madaket Mall."

the art of collecting

My friends Jimmie Cramer and Dean Johnson have some of the best collections I know of, and not one of them is anything you might find in a museum, a book, or an auction catalog. They are masters of collecting the functional, and turning it, by virtue of repetition and thoughtful display, into art. They have an eye for seeing sculpture in workaday tools and quirky components that others might pass right by. For example, they collect objects as diverse as old hose nozzles and sprinklers, flower frogs and garden markers, old clock numerals, iron fence ornaments, and hefty, well-used pliers. In their potting shed, the collections turn to watering cans of a bright-green hue, old glass garden cloches, and miniature trellises. Grouped together, with space to reveal their intriguing silhouettes and patinated finishes, they have a freshness and vitality that eclipses more expected collections. Finding something that captivates you *before* it becomes a hot collectible, or seeking out a common denominator among items you already own, can be a very affordable way to animate empty walls, spark a bare mantel—or a conversation.

By the same token, items that were intended as collectibles can still have charm today, especially when they're massed in large numbers, or taken out of context. Tacky miniatures of the Statue of Liberty, Empire State Building, or other tourist destinations make an irrepressibly fun skyline across a mantel. Souvenir plates from world's fairs and other events can be grouped on a wall or

Green is the theme for a collection of emerald-bright watering cans, flower pots, and a berry basket in the potting shed. Weathered baskets hung from a branch hold raffia and twine.

The sculptural shapes of old lawn sprinklers and pruning shears give these collections of time-blackened tools a utilitarian beauty. They could be hung on a kitchen wall, displayed on shelves, or in some cases, pressed into active duty.

used to catch spare change. The next step up is memorabilia like trophies and loving cups, or look for something going out of style, like tabletop cigarette lighters. The key to affordable collecting is to buy things ahead of the curve or apart from the trends; the moment an item becomes hot, whether it's globes or Indian clubs, it becomes expensive or gets knocked off by a manufacturer. Choose something that is affordable enough that you can buy one or two as you find them, so that over time you've acquired a worthwhile collection.

Broken off and rusted, iron fence ornaments become interesting forms in their own right. En masse, the mundane becomes mesmerizing, like the quirky perforated shapes and swirls of metal flower frogs, **left.**

The least likely
of collections—
old hose nozzles—
forms a wonderful
frieze lined up
along a beam in a
garden shed. The
distinctive silhou-
ettes are backlit
by sunbeams
filtering through
corrugated glass.

Old globes reflect political as well as personal history, and are still easy to find at garage sales; here, they add a worldly touch to metal shelving. Heart-shaped milagros, **right,** bestow a romantic gleam on a dark, painted-wood screen that has the visual impact of a headboard.

Sometimes collections do more than just look good: These large, round wooden finials happen to make perfect hat forms. They are at home in the bedroom beneath a peg rail that holds a mirror and towels or clothes.

Plan of Attack
Finding the Bargains at a Flea Market

While some of the biggest markets, such as the one in Brimfield, Massachusetts, have become so famous that they offer few bargains, smaller ones still provide the best opportunity to find a wide range of well-priced merchandise. After decades of trudging through flea markets, this is my plan of attack:

• **Arrive as early as possible. Although serious sleuthers peer into the backs of trucks with flashlights before daybreak, your best bet is probably to see a piece in the light of day, where you can examine its condition and determine if it works for you.**

• **Go with a list of what you're looking for so you won't be sidetracked into making unnecessary purchases. You want to be open to serendipity, but buying something you have no real use for is never a bargain.**

• **Get a map of the dealers, if possible, and target your first visits to any you already know and like. Otherwise, follow an orderly route so you can keep track of where you've been. If you find dealers you like, get their business cards and sign their mailing lists so you can find them at future shows.**

• **Don't rush into a purchase: Stake your claim by holding onto items you're interested in, but take time to evaluate a piece before making an offer. If it is a piece of furniture, check how well it is constructed: Open the drawers of a bureau or desk, look at the joints, and test the ease of operation. Look at the undersides of chairs and tables to see if the legs have been changed or added. Check for repairs, cracks, mismatched pieces of wood. Sit in a chair and test its solidity. Note if signs of wear are in logical places (around knobs and edges) or seem to be faked.**

• **If you're new to collecting, look at lots of booths (and lots of markets) to get a feel for pricing, or check price guides for well-known collectibles. Learn by asking questions of knowledgeable dealers when they're not too busy; many are happy to share their expertise.**

• **Don't be afraid to bargain, but don't offer the dealer an insultingly low price. A good approach is to say, "Can you do any better on this?" or "How about—" offering a price 10 to 20 percent below asking. If you are buying several pieces from one dealer, or you notice any flaws in the piece, you will have more leverage for negotiating. Offering cash always brings the best price.**

• **If you can't go early, stay late: That's often the best time to make a deal, when dealers would rather lower their prices than have more to pack up and ship home.**

These Statue of Liberty souvenir figurines might be dismissed by most "serious" collectors, yet gathered on a mantel, in all their minute variety, they have considerable charm.

A pile of vintage cushions runs the gamut from handsome stripes to homey words of wisdom inscribed on a balsam-filled souvenir pillow.

100 smart tricks

1. Hang an extra-large chalkboard in any room and let a changing gallery of spontaneous art (or to-do lists) decorate the walls.

2. Don't hide all your Christmas ornaments away after the holidays: Fill a glass bowl with sparkling balls or hang favorite ornaments from cupboard pulls or doorknobs.

3. Looking for something novel and inexpensive to frame? Consider using playing cards; menus from memorable meals; calendar pictures; a collage of old ticket stubs; labels from canned goods, seed packages, or wine bottles; art postcards; subway or road maps; theater programs; greeting cards; CD or record album covers.

4. Découpage any of the above on a wide wooden picture or mirror frame, or place them beneath a sheet of glass on a coffee table for a changeable collage.

5. Color copy old photographs and glue them to a tray or tabletop, then polyurethane them to protect them from spills.

6. Hang mirrors or pictures with wide, heavy velvet or silk ribbon tied into an oversized bow.

7. Add contemporary or vintage knobs to an old dresser to give it a new look.

8. Instead of covering a window with a full curtain, use a valance alone.

9. Use lengths of wide ribbon on top of a tablecloth to add seasonal color.

10. Use different sets of slipcovers for throw pillows to give a quick winter/summer makeover to a room.

11. Use inexpensive "checkerboard" vinyl tiles to re-cover a floor, then stencil the lighter squares with a decorative motif.

12. Make an alcove look like a closet by hanging a curtain, or hang a roller shade over a bookshelf to conceal storage.

13. Decant dishwashing soap and laundry detergent into pretty glass bottles (old wine or olive oil bottles, for example).

14. Adorn the tops of paintings or mirrors

with fresh greens any time of year;
give a statue or bust a small leafy wreath.

15. Use nautical hardware such as cleats for window treatments.

16. Hang finished puzzles (affixed with puzzle glue) or colorful old game boards on the wall.

17. Decorate bookshelves or a mantel with toys that belonged to you or your children.

18. Frame a mirror with real or artifical ivy or millinery leaves.

19. Glue old buttons to pushpins to dress up your bulletin board.

20. Use a retail postcard or magazine rack (sometimes available at thrift shops or free for the picking on the street) to hold correspondence and magazines.

21. Old fur or faux fur stoles (often cheap at secondhand stores) make great throws on chairs or a sofa.

22. Use new or vintage house numbers or wooden or metal sign letters instead of place cards at the table, or hang them on the wall or set them on a shelf.

23. An assemblage of house plants, can-

dles, or magazines always looks more attractive organized on a tray.

24. Tie sets of sheets together in your linen closet with pretty ribbons. Do the same with bundles of letters and cards you want to save.

25. Tie a stack of books together with wide ribbon or heavy twine.

26. Cover buttons on a tufted chair or ottoman with different fabrics.

27. Use an old wooden ladder as a bookshelf by stacking books on each step, or for displaying quilts or linens.

28. Swap standard knobs for novel drawer pulls in a kitchen or any room by using forks, knives, and spoons, small twigs, shells, game pieces, pieces of sturdy cord or rope, or dice.

29. Use wallpaper remnants to cover a box or line drawers.

30. Install a narrow shelf high on the wall all the way around the room and use it to display a collection of similar, inexpensive objects, such as rocks, seashells, and glass jars.

31. Plant fast-growing paperwhites in stones and water, in almost any con-

tainer, for winter-long continuous display and fragrance.

32. Stack attractive towels on an open rack in the bathroom instead of concealing them in the linen closet.

33. Make color photocopies of prints and pictures from books and magazines to frame or use for decoupaging tables, lampshades, chests, and such.

34. Use jewelry—bracelets, jeweled pins, necklaces—as napkin rings.

35. Anchor a pillar candle in an urn or flowerpot filled with nuts, small Christmas balls, coffee beans or shells.

36. Place a battery-operated string of tiny white lights inside a glass bowl or vase for glowing year-round decoration.

37. Hang children's artwork or favorite postcards or photos with clothespins on a clothesline hung on the wall.

38. Stack books, magazines or newspapers to form a "side table" by the sofa or bed (if you like, you can formalize this arrangement with a glass top cut to fit).

39. Use bandanas to cover throw pillows, or sew them together to make casual café curtains.

40. Hang cookie cutters, old utensils, tools or garden implements on a kitchen wall.

41. Use ribbon, lace or paper doilies to edge shelves in a linen closet or cupboard.

42. For a distinctive lamp base, try wiring a pottery vase, magnum wine bottle, wooden baluster, trophy or glass jar.

43. Look for cheap storage stowaways at a toy store, five-and-dime, or hardware store: colorful metal sand pails, plastic boxes and bins, galvanized metal boxes and pails, wooden crates and buckets.

44. Strings of Christmas lights, Japanese lanterns or paper-bag luminarias provide inexpensive outdoor lighting.

45. Strip the paint off old metal office furniture and file cabinets for the brushed steel look that's currently so popular and pricey.

46. Paint a "mirror" or "clock" face on the wall for whimsical wall art.

47. Stencil a favorite saying or names around a room as a frieze.

48. Tack crisscrossed ribbons to the inside of an armoire or cupboard door to form a memory board.

49. Save broken china and pottery shards

and use them to form a mosaic on a flowerpot, frame, tabletop, or backsplash.

50. Rescue orphaned glasses or crystal goblets for vases, bath or bedroom water glasses, or to hold odds and ends.

51. Bring garden figures, planters, or even summer furniture indoors in the winter to use as decoration.

52. Use fabric markers to write each person's name on a tablecloth to mark their "place" at the table.

53. Reincarnate old shutters as interior window shutters.

54. Make lots of photocopies of a set of botanical prints and use them to paper a bedroom or bath.

55. Organize odds and ends such as matchbooks, film canisters, paper clips, and business cards in glass fishbowls or apothecary jars.

56. Put branches or pieces of driftwood to use as shelf supports or a table base, or to frame a mirror.

57. Frame pages from a children's book to decorate a baby's room.

58. Stock up on inexpensive director's chairs, folding metal French park chairs, or bamboo chairs for portable, stowaway extra seating.

59. Spray pinecones and faux millinery fruits with a dash of gold or silver and mix with metal balls in a bowl or terra-cotta pot.

60. Camouflage stains on slipcovers and bedspreads with patches of hearts or squares in pretty floral fabrics.

61. Unify disparate objects by color—mass all-white or clear-glass pitchers, candlesticks, vases, and platters together in an arrangement.

62. Organize your kitchen with a peg-rack display of metal utensils such as colanders, graters, whisks and strainers.

63. Wooden pallets, cable spools and packing crates can be reclaimed as coffee tables, end tables, or bookshelves.

64. Personalize throw pillows, towels, or napkins with a single, oversize initial monogram.

65. Frame a graphic piece of fabric or a sheet of wallpaper or wrapping paper.

66. Wallpaper a single wall in a strong print that might be overwhelming in a whole room.

67. Paint kitchen cabinets or part of a child's room wall with blackboard paint, then let them scribble to their heart's content.

68. Have a motif photo-transferred onto fabric, which can be done at places that make photo T-shirts, for throw pillows or napkins.

69. Add designer detail to ready-made sheets or curtains with ribbon, braid, or buttons.

70. Cover a wall with homasote (found at building supply and home centers) and then paint or cover with fabric to make a giant bulletin board.

71. Make coordinating fabric roller shades yourself with iron-on kits available at sewing stores.

72. Use doorknobs, cabinet pulls, large shells, or finials as holdbacks for curtains.

73. Salvage clothes you no longer wear by using them to make pillows or quilts. Scarves and wraps can become throws.

74. Cover sturdy cardboard storage boxes with wallpaper or fabric that will coordinate with a bedroom. Add grosgrain ribbon ties.

75. Extend a set of china or patterned plates by mixing them with inexpensive plain white or clear glass tableware.

76. For cheap floor coverings use straw or tatami (beach) mats, a painted canvas floor cloth, or rag rugs.

77. Bind industrial carpeting, sisal or a carpet remnant with contrasting twill tape to create an inexpensive area rug.

78. Cover an inexpensive chipboard or fiberboard chest with wallpaper.

79. Inexpensive headboard possibilities: a piece of trellis, an iron gate, picket fencing, or old shutters, or use a flag, wall hanging, vintage tablecloth, area rug, or painting to serve as a visual "headboard."

80. Make a fabric slipcover for an unattractive wood or iron headboard.

81. Instead of one large rug, create a patchwork of small rugs by securing them on the undersides with carpet tape.

82. Turn a small room into a library by covering the walls with bookshelves. Unfinished shelves are generally inexpensive and can be painted or varnished or left as is.

83. Paint stair risers a softer color for a subtle change of pace.

84. Use a reversible bedcover for a quick room makeover.

85. Tuck photos and mementos into a piece of wire garden fence or wooden trellis.

86. Recycle old bed pillows as oversize throw pillows or cushions; recycle old down comforters as featherbeds.

87. Create an oversize mirror by framing a large piece of mirrored glass with wood molding bought at the lumberyard.

88. Inexpensive room dividers: hang curtains or bamboo blinds, or use a set of bookshelves or a screen.

89. Make a screen from old or new doors, shutters, or fabric panels stretched on a wood frame.

90. Add inexpensive molding to ready-made bookshelves to give them more depth and character.

91. Wallpaper or paint the inside of a cupboard or bookshelves a strong color for a rich surprise.

92. Add a picture rail, chair rail, crown molding, or deeper baseboards to give a plain room architectural detail.

93. Combine stock moldings to create more elaborate profiles.

94. Use an old window as the front for a cupboard or as the frame for a picture or mirror.

95. Instead of installing new kitchen cabinets, make your current ones more functional with the addition of pot and lid racks, dish racks, hanging glass racks, cup hooks, lazy Susans, and stepped shelves.

96. Have old appliances professionally spray-painted for a new look (try auto body shops or medical equipment suppliers).

97. Add glass-front or chicken-wire doors to old kitchen cabinets to lighten them up. Or, if you don't want to see what's inside, shirr fabric panels across the front.

98. Stencil a design or border using wood stain on a wooden floor to give the look of parquet at a fraction of the price.

99. Use hanging wire kitchen baskets and iron plate racks to creatively organize papers and projects at a desk.

100. Request fabric samples or "memos" from fabric companies when possible; they're perfect for covering throw pillows.

directory

Resources for Smart Decorating

Arizona

The Brass Armadillo
12419 North 28th Drive
Interstate 17,
north of Cactus Road
Phoenix, AZ 85029
888-942-0030
This 40,000-square-foot antique mall hosts close to 600 dealers of architectural elements, lighting, furniture, and small items.

Phoenix Fairgrounds Antiques Market
State Fairgrounds
1826 West McDowell
Phoenix, AZ 85007
602-943-1766
This year-round monthly antiques and collectibles show is held on Saturday and Sunday, the third weekend of the month.

Arkansas

James L. Couch Antiques
PO Box 251391
Little Rock, AR 72225
501-374-4793
Shop sells 18th- and 19th-century English and French country furniture and decorative accessories. By appointment only.

Potential Treasures Antiques
700 North Van Buren Street
Little Rock, AR 72205
501-663-0608
Shop sells traditional 19th- and 20th-century antiques, including linens, mirrors, sterling, and china.

California

About Antiques
3533 Ocean View Boulevard
Glendale, CA 91208
818-249-8587
Antique shop sells textiles, decorative accessories, and pottery.

Alabaster
597 Hayes Street
San Francisco, CA 94102
415-558-0482
Shop sells eclectic antiques such as alabaster, hotel silverware, cake stands, and white ironstone.

Areo
207 Ocean Avenue
Laguna Beach, CA 92651
949-376-0535
Shop specializes in new and antique gifts and home accessories.

Bountiful
1335 Abbot Kinney Boulevard
Venice, CA 90291
310-450-3620
This large shop sells primitive American painted furniture,18th- and 19th-century French furniture and accessories, French and Italian lighting, French leather club chairs, and architectural elements.

F. Dorian, Inc.
388 Hayes Street
San Francisco, CA 94102
415-861-3191
Shop sells ethnic art, world crafts, and jewelry.

Hyde & Seek Antiques
1913 Hyde Street
San Francisco, CA 94109
415-776-8865
Shop sells antique quilts and paisleys, old American Indian rugs and blankets, Mexican silver, bakelite jewelry, tramp art, and folk art.

Interieur Perdu
340 Bryant Street/2nd Street
San Francisco, CA 94107
415-543-1616
Shop sells antique French furniture and accessories.

James "JC" Connors
564 Hayes Street
San Francisco, CA 94102
415-558-6904
Shop sells collectibles, antique toys, and housewares.

Liz's Antique Hardware
453 South La Brea
Los Angeles, CA 90036
323-939-4403
www.LAHardware.com
Sells anything and everything when it comes to decorative hardware. Also has a matching service.

Newport Avenue Antique Center
4864 Newport Avenue
San Diego, CA 92107
619-222-8686
Antique mall holds 170 dealers with a variety of antiques and collectibles.

Rose Bowl Flea Market and Swap Meet
Pasadena Rose Bowl
1001 Rose Bowl Drive
Pasadena, CA 91103
323-560-7469
More than 2,200 dealers sell everything from antiques to crafts. Open the second Sunday of each month.

Santa Monica Antique Market
1607 Lincoln Boulevard
Santa Monica, CA 90404
310-314-4899
Over 150 dealers display variety of antiques and collectibles including sporting memorabilia and gardening items.

Swallow Tail
2217 Polk Street
San Francisco, CA 94109
415-567-1555
Sells Victorian to 1930's antiques and architectural salvage.

Treasure Island Flea Market
415 255-1923
www.treasureisland
   market.com
Rain or shine, this Sunday-only flea market offers all types of antiques, collectibles and other treasures.

Wild Goose Chase Antique Americana
31521 Camino Capistrano #A
San Juan, CA 92675
949-487-2720
Shop sells antique Americana, quilts, Beacon blankets, pre-1900 antiques and painted furniture.

Zonal
2139 Polk Street
San Francisco, CA 94109
415-563-2220

568 Hayes Street
San Francisco, CA 94102
415-255-9307
www.zonalhome.com
Shops sell American country painted furniture, turn-of-the-century iron beds, and architectural artifacts.

Colorado

Alderfer's Antiques
309 East Main Street
Aspen, CO 81611
970-925-5051
Shop sells Beacon blankets, jewelry, and western accessories.

The Great Camp Collection Sherwood Design Company
358 Main Street
Carbondale, CO 81623
970-963-0221
Shop sells western furniture and Beacon blankets.

West Antiques
401/409 S. Public Road
Lafayette, CO 80026
303-666-7200
This 13,000 square foot shop specializes in antique furniture and accessories.

Connecticut

Balcony Antique Shops
81 Albany Turnpike,
Route 44
Canton, CT 06019
860-693-4478
Sells eclectic antique accessories.

Sweethaven Farm
Academy Street
Salisbury, CT 06068
860-435-6064
Specializes in garden artistry and vintage wares. Seasonal, call for hours.

Woodbury Outdoor Market
Intersection of
  Routes 6 and 64
Woodbury, CT 06798
203-263-2841
Antique sale and flea market event happens most Saturday mornings year-round.

Delaware

Bargain Bill's Antique & Flea Market
Intersection of Routes 13 and 9
Laurel, DE 19956
302-875-2478
Two hundred indoor booths and 300 outdoor tables make up this year-round weekend flea market.

Bellefonte Resale Shop
901 Brandywine Blvd.
Wilmington, DE 19802
302-762-1885
Shop sells miscellaneous items such as antiques clocks and oil lamps.

Twice Nice Antiques
5714 Kennett Pike
Centreville, DE 19807
302-656-8881
Shop sells Chippendale, Federal, and Queen Anne furnishings and accessories.

District of Columbia

Georgetown Flea Market
Wisconsin Avenue between S and T
  Streets NW
Washington, DC 20007
202-296-4989
www.georgetown.com
This antiques and collectibles only flea market happens on Sundays, March through Christmas.

Antiques Anonymous
2627 Connecticut Avenue NW
Washington, DC 20008
202-332-5555
Sells eclectic small 19th- and 20th-century antiques and jewelry.

Michael Getz Antiques
2918 M Street NW
Washington, DC 20007
202-338-3811
Shop sells silver, fireplace accessories, lamps, and china.

Florida

Joseph's Antiques
616 Green Street
Key West, FL 33040
305-292-1333
Offers marine antiques.

Renningers Florida Twin Markets
20651 US Highway 441
Mt. Dora, FL 32757-1699
352-383-8393
Two separate markets reside on 115 acres; one antiques, one a farmers and flea market. Open Saturday and Sunday year-round.

The Shell Warehouse
Mallory Square
#1 Whitehead Street
Key West, FL 33040
305-294-5168
Sells shells and corals of all types.

Webster Westside Flea Market
Corner of County Road
  478 and Northwest
  3rd Street
Webster, FL 33597
800-832-7396
Dubbed "Antiques Alley," this flea market is open every Monday morning.

Wisteria Corner Antique Mall
225 North Main Street
High Springs, FL 32643
904-454-3555
Shop sells American and European antiques, collectibles, and handcrafted items.

Georgia

Atlanta Antiques Exchange
1185 Howell Mill
  Road NW
Atlanta, GA 30318
404-351-0727
Sells a large variety of 19th- and 20th-century English, Oriental, and Continental pottery and porcelain.

Interiors Market
55 Bennett Street
  NW #20
Atlanta, GA 30309
404-352-0055
Around 40 dealers sell a variety of French and English antiques and decorative accessories.

Jacqueline Adams Antiques
2300 Peachtree Road
  NW, Suite #B110
Atlanta, GA 30309
404-355-8123
Shop sells an assortment of French country antiques and decorative accessories.

Levison & Cullen Gallery
2300 Peachtree Road
Suite #C102
Atlanta, GA 30309
404-351-3435
Shop sells American antiques and decorative art from the 18th and 19th centuries.

The Stalls
116 Bennett Street
Atlanta, GA 30309
404-352-4430
This antique market hosts 60 dealers of all types of antiques and collectibles.

Idaho

WaterLemon
305 East Park Street,
Suite #403
McCall, ID 83638
208-634-2529
Shop sells American country antiques.

Illinois

Kane County Flea Market
Kane County
   Fairgrounds
Randall Road between
   Routes 64 and 38
St. Charles, IL 60174
630-377-2252
As many as 1,400 dealers sell their wares the first Sunday of every month and the preceding Saturday afternoon.

McCormick Art & Antiques
214 W. St. Louis St.
Lebanon, IL 62254
618-667-7789
Shop features fine American painted furniture, antique folk art, quilts, rugs, and architectural items.

3rd Sunday Market
Interstate Center at the
   McLean County
   Fairgrounds
Bloomington, IL 61761
309-452-7926
Some 450 dealers sell at this indoor and outdoor market. Open third Sunday of the month, May through November.

Turtle Creek Antiques
850 West Armitage
   Avenue
Chicago, IL 60614
773-327-2630
Shop sells vintage fabrics and linens, antique quilts, and estate jewelry.

Indiana

Indianapolis Downtown Antiques
1044 Virginia Avenue
Indianapolis, IN 46203
317-635-5336
Forty dealers sell antique furniture, depression glass, American art pottery, and blue and white stoneware.

Webb's Antique Mall
200 West Union Street
Centerville, IN 47330
765-855-5542
Antique mall hosts more than 500 dealers of eclectic an-tiques and collectibles.

Iowa

The Brass Armadillo
701 Northeast 50th
   Avenue
Des Moines, IA 50313
515-262-0092
Antique mall houses 400 dealers.

Collectors Paradise Flea Market
Keokuk County
   Fairgrounds
What Cheer, IA 50268
515-634-2109
Indoor/outdoor market runs the first weekend in May, August, and October.

Majestic Lion Antique Center
5048 2nd Avenue
Des Moines, IA 50313
515-282-5466
Antique mall with close to 250 dealers offers a variety of antiques and collectibles.

Kansas

Jeanette McVay's Prairie Primitives
1833 North 134th Street
Kansas City, KS 66109
913-721-2511
Sells various items, including concrete garden pumpkins, papier mâché boxes, chalkware, and penny rugs.

Old World Antiques Ltd.
4436 State Line Road
Kansas City, KS 66103
913-677-4744
Sells French Old World antiques and accessories.

Mid-America Flea Markets
PO Box 1585
Hutchinson, KS 67504
316-663-5626
Close to 600 dealers convene one Sunday a month, September through June. Call for details.

Kentucky

Steve White Gallery
945 Baxter Avenue
Louisville, KY 40204
502-458-9581
Shop sells period antiques.

Kentucky Flea Market
Kentucky Fair and
   Expo Center
Junction of Interstates
   264 and 65
Louisville, KY 40220
502-456-2244
www.stewartpromo-tions.com
This large flea market hosts between 1,000 and 2,000 dealers one weekend a month.

Ruth C. Scully Antiques
Louisville, KY 40291
502-491-9601

Shop sells early 19th century furniture, decorative arts, textiles, and folk art. By appointment only.

Louisiana

Mac Maison, Ltd.
3963 Magazine Street
New Orleans, LA 70115
504-891-2863
Shop sells antiques, architectural artifacts, lighting, and ornamentations.

Jefferson Flea Market
5501 Jefferson Highway
Harahan, LA 70183
504-734-0087
Seventy to seventy-five dealers sell antiques and collectibles every Friday through Sunday.

Maine

The Maples
424 Bristol Road
Bristol, ME 04539
207-563-2645
Shop sells country primitives and folk art.

The Marston House
Main Street
Wiscasset, ME 04578
207-882-6010
Shop sells primarily late 18th- and 19-century American painted furniture and accessories, textiles, and garden antiques.

Riverbank Antiques
Wells Union Antique
   Center on Rural
   Route 1
Wells, ME 07090
207-646-6314
Mall of 80 dealers sells English, French, and Italian garden architectural elements and decorative antiques. Seasonal, call for hours.

Wales & Hamblen Antique Center
134 Main Street
Bridgton, ME 04009
207-647-3840
A small co-op of 38 dealers who specialize in small antiques. Open Memorial Day through October.

Maryland

All of Us Americana Folk Art
5530 Pembroke Road
Bethesda, MD 20817
301-652-4626
Shop specializes in quilts and American Indian jewelry and fetishes.

Annapolis Antique Shop
27 Riverview Avenue
Annapolis, MD 21401
410-266-5550
Shop sells eclectic antiques and consignment items.

Beaver Creek Antique Market
20202 National Pike
Hagerstown, MD 21740
301-739-8075
An antique market of 150 dealers offers eclectic collectibles.

Edward & Edward, The Consignment Warehouse
35 South Carroll Street
Frederick, MD 21701
301-695-9674
Houses antiques, decorative arts, architectural and garden items.

Great Stuff by Paul
10 North Carroll Street
Frederick, MD 21701
301-631-0004
Shop sells garden, galvanized, wooden, and architectural decorative accessories.

Olsen's Furniture & Antiques, Inc.
31648 Curtis Chapel Rd.
Westover, MD 21871
410-957-1650
This shop sells a large variety of antiques and used furniture.

Massachusetts

Brimfield Antiques Market
Route 20
Brimfield, MA 01010
413-245-7479
Open three times a year (May, July, and September), this enormous antiques flea market actually consists of 22 markets and hosts between 3,000 and 4,000 dealers.

Charles River Antiques
45 River Street
Boston, MA 02108
617-367-3244
Shop sells rustic antiques.

Essentials
88 Main Street
N. Hampton, MA 01060
413-584-2327
Shop sells new upholstered furniture, gift wrap, paper goods.

Nantucket Country
38 Centre Street
Nantucket, MA 02554
508-228-8868
Antique shop carries quilts and collectibles.

Michigan

Great Midwestern Antique Emporium
5233 Dixie Highway
Waterford, MI 48329
248-623-7460
Co-op antique mall houses 50 dealers of antiques and collectibles including pottery and furniture.

Kalik's Antiques
198 West Liberty
Plymouth, MI 48170
734-455-5595
Eight dealers specialize in furniture and military, western, sports, hunting, and fishing antiques.

Rage of the Age
314 South Ashley Street
Ann Arbor, MI 48104
734-662-0777
Shop sells vintage clothing and textiles.

Slightly Tarnished-Used Goods
2006 East Michigan Avenue
Lansing, MI 48912
517-485-3599
Shop sells a variety of used goods, including antique lamps and furniture.

Minnesota

Antiques Minnesota
1197 University Avenue
St. Paul, MN 55104
651-646-0037
Antique mall hosts 90 dealers of glassware, pottery, ceramics, furniture, jewelry, and toys.

Wescott Station
226 West Seventh Street
St. Paul, MN 55102
651-227-2469
Shop sells vintage framed artwork, pottery, stained glass, furniture, lamps, platters, etc.

Mississippi

Bobbieking Antiques & Interiors
667 Dulling Avenue
Woodland Hills Shopping Center
Jackson, MS 39216
601-362-9803
Shop sells antique and contemporary linens, jewelry, accessories.

Missouri

Antiques & More
2309 Cherokee Street
St. Louis, MO 63118
314-773-1150
Shop sells miscellaneous antiques and collectibles.

Heart of Country Antiques Show
427 Midvale Avenue
St. Louis, MO 63130
800-862-1090
www.heartofcountry.com
Held on Valentine's weekend and again in October, the best in country primitives is available.

Missouri Plain Folk
Sikeston, MO 63801
573-471-6949
Dealers specialize in rural Americana. By appointment only.

Montana

Depot Antique Mall
2223 Montana Avenue
Billings, MT 59101
406-245-5955
Over 60 dealers specialize in antiques and collectibles.

Nebraska

The Brass Armadillo
10666 Sapp Brothers Drive
Omaha, NE 68138
800-896-9140
Large antique mall hosts 350 dealers.

Flea Market Emporium
3235 South 13th Street
Lincoln, NE 68502
402-423-5380
An antique mall with over 50 dealers sells a variety of antiques and collectibles.

Nevada

Frontier Antique Mall
221 South Curry Street
Carson City, NV 89703
702-887-1466
Dealers sell all
kinds of antiques
and collectibles.

**Red Rooster Antiques
and Collectibles Mall**
1109 Western Avenue
Las Vegas, NV 89102
702-382-5253
Sixty dealers sell an-
tique lighting fixtures,
lamps, and other mis-
cellaneous antiques.

New Hampshire

**Burlwood
Antique Center**
106 Daniel Webster
   Highway
Meredith, NH 03253
603-279-6387
Open only May through
October, this market
has an entire floor of
furniture as well as
other antiques and
collectibles.

**Bert Savage
Larch Lodge**
Route 126
Ctr. Strafford, NH 03815
603-269-7411
Sells antique rustic fur-
niture and accessories.
By appointment only.

**Colonial Antiques &
Flea Market**
Route 12A
West Lebanon, NH 03784
603-298-7712
This daily market has
over 65 dealers that sell
a variety of antiques,
collectibles, and all
types of other old stuff.

New Jersey

**Americana
by the Seashore**
604 Broadway
Barnegat Light, NJ 08006
609-494-0656
Shop sells antique
furniture, glassware,
quilts, pillows, and
pictures.

**Golden Nugget
Antique and Flea
Market**
State Hwy. 29
Lambertville, NJ 08530
609-397-0811
Forty antique shops are
open Saturday and
Sunday; an outdoor flea
market is open
Wednesday, Saturday,
and Sunday.

The Drawing Room
36 South Main Street
Lambertville, NJ 08530
609-397-7977
Sells 18th- and 19th-
century English and
Continental furniture
and accessories.

**Lambertville Antique
Flea Market**
1864 River Road
Lambertville, NJ 08530
609-397-0456
Close to 150 dealers
sell antiques and
collectibles every
Wednesday, Saturday,
and Sunday.

New Mexico

Antiques & Alike
3904 Central Avenue SE
Alburquerque, NM 87108
505-268-1882
Shop sells antique
furniture, lighting, and
accessories.

**Cowboys & Indians
Antiques**
4000 Central Ave. SE
Alburquerque, NM 87108
505-255-4054
Antique shop special-
izes in pre-1940s
American Indian items
and pre-1950s Western
memorbilia.

**Pegasus Antiques
& Collectibles**
Santa Fe, NM
505-982-3333
Shop sells miscella-
neous antiques, includ-
ing Southwestern. By
appointment only.

**Pueblo of Tesuque
Flea Market**
Highway 285, approxi-
   mately 7 miles north of
   Santa Fe
505-983-2667 or
   505-660-8948
Flea market deals most
Friday, Saturday, and
Sunday, May through
September; open
Saturdays and Sundays
during March and April.

The Rainbow Man
107 East Palace Avenue
Santa Fe, NM 87501
505-982-8706
Shop sells new and old
American Indian items,
folk art, and photogra-
phy of the Southwest.

New York

**Annyx
A Matter of Taste**
150 Main Street
Sag Harbor, NY 11963
516-725-9064
Shop sells old and new
collectibles. Seasonal,
call for hours.

**Barbara Trujillo
Antiques
Kinneman &
Ramaekers
Nancy Boyd**
2466 Main Street
PO Box 866
Bridgehampton, NY
   11932
516-537-3838
Several dealers sell
American country primi-
tive antiques, holiday-
themed antiques, and
Mexican and Indian
jewelry. Seasonal, call
for hours.

Bagley Home
155 Main Street
Sag Harbor, NY 11963
516-725-3553
Shop sells painted fur-
niture, vintage kitchen
accessories, and lots of
linens. Seasonal, call
for hours.

Copake Auction Inc.
Box H, Route 22 to 260
   Route 7A
Copake, NY 12516
518-329-1142
www.copakeauc-
tion.com
Company hosts a
monthly Americana
auction along with
other various auctions.

Covington Candle
976 Lexington Avenue
New York, NY 10021
212-472-1131
Shop sells all shapes
and sizes of candles.

**English Country
Antiques**
Snake Hollow Road
Bridgehampton, NY
   11932
516-537-0606
Shop sells English
country antiques
including furniture,
china, and baskets.

Fishs Eddy
Broadway & 19th Street
New York, NY 10003
212-420-9020
www.fishseddy.com
Three locations sell
vintage and new
restaurant-style
tableware.

Hunters & Collectors
Montauk Highway and
    Poxabogue Lane
Bridgehampton, NY
    11932
516-537-4233
Shop specializes in
country and modern
furniture, reupholstered
furniture, bowls, and
lamps.

La Tienda
50 Spring Street
New York, NY 10012
212-431-4404
Shop sells silver mila-
gros and other old and
new Mexican decora-
tive accessories.

Laura Fisher
1050 Second Avenue
Gallery 84
New York, NY 10022
212-838-2596
This gallery shop is the
source for antique
quilts, hooked rugs, and
other textiles.

Olde Good Things
124 West 24th Street
New York, NY 10011
212-989-8401
Shop specializes in sal-
vage architectural arti-
facts such as columns,
gates, fences, door-
knobs, mantels, and
tubs as well as door
and window hardware.

**Pageant Book &
Print Shop**
114 West Houston Street
New York, NY 10012
212-674-5296
Shop stocks a large
selection of old maps,
documents, books, and
other papers.

Paris Images
170 Bleecker Street
New York, NY 10012
212-473-7552

Sells vintage and
reproduction posters
and postcards. Also
contemporary and vin-
tage framing.

Paula Rubenstein Ltd.
65 Prince Street
New York, NY 10012
212-966-8954
Shop sells vintage pais-
leys, quilts, and Beacon
blankets and antique
accessories.

Potted Gardens
27 Bedford Street
New York, NY 10014
212-255-4797
Garden-influenced fur-
niture, garden statuary,
and antique garden
accessories. Also has
a flower and garden
design service.

Rhubarb Home
26 Bond Street
New York, NY 10012
212-533-1817
Store offers eclectic
cottage furnishings,
including their own line
of home furnishings,
such as metal-topped
tables and dog beds.

Ruby Beets Antiques
1703 Montauk Highway
Bridgehampton, NY
516-537-2802
Situated in a house, this
antique shop sells an
eclectic mix of painted
furniture and decorative
accessories. Seasonal,
call for hours.

Sage Street Antiques
Corner of Route 114 and
    Sage Street
Sag Harbor, NY 11963
516-725-4036
Open only on weekends,
this small shop sells a
variety of antiques
including kitchen col-
lectibles, linens, framed
antique prints, ceram-
ics, and other treasures
at yard-sale prices.

Solomon's Mine
95 Main Street
Cold Springs, NY 10516
914-265-5042
Shop sells unique
antiques and collectibles
like cameras and old
medical equipment.

Strand Bookstore
828 Broadway at 12th
    Street
New York, NY 10003
212-473-1452
Store filled floor to ceiling with new and used
books on all subjects.

**Ted Meyer's
Harbor Antiques**
Montauk Highway
Wainscott, NY 11975
516-537-1442
Shop stocks a large
selection of wicker fur-
niture and iron beds.
Also sells some antique
accessories. Seasonal,
call for hours.

**The Annex: Antiques
Fair and Flea Market**
26th Street and Avenue
    of the Americas
New York, NY
    10116-4627
212-243-5343
Flea market happens
every Saturday and
Sunday. Also visit The
Garage across the
avenue on 25th Street.

The Whatnot Shop
525 Warren Street
Hudson, NY 12534
518-828-1081
Shop sells eclectic
antiques.

North Carolina

The Farmer's Wife
339 South Davie Street
Greensboro, NC 27401
336-274-7920
Antique shop sells
architectural salvage,
baskets, framed prints,
and garden items.

Metrolina Expo
7100 Statesville Road
Charlotte, NC 28269
704-596-4643 or
800-824-3770
One weekend of every
month is devoted to
antiques and collectibles
at this large market.

Parker's Trading Post
1051 US Highway 17 S
Elizabeth City, NC 27909
252-335-4896
Shop sells odd and
unusual antiques and
collectibles.

North Dakota

Wizard of Odds 'N Ends
1523 East Thayer Avenue
Bismarck, ND 58501
701-222-4175
Sells antique
accessories.

Ohio

**America Antiques and
Emporium**
26 South Third Street
Newark, OH 43055
740-345-0588
Shops offers three
floors of primitive
antiques.

Antiques Etcetera Mall
3265 North High Street
Columbus, OH 43202
614-447-2242
Antique mall of 20 deal-
ers offers primitive fur-
niture, pottery, and
Southwestern jewelry.

M. Dallas
PO Box 278
Danville, OH 43104
740-599-5919
Shop sells "Old Glory"
flag dinnerware and
antique reproduction
spatterware.

Springfield Antique Show and Flea Market
Clark County
   Fairgrounds, Exit 59 off
   Interstate 70
4401 South Charleston
   Pike
Springfield, OH 45501
937-325-0053
Around 1,200 dealers
market antique and collectibles one weekend
each month.

Oklahoma

AMC Flea Market Mall
1001 North Pennsylvania
   Avenue
Oklahoma City, OK
   73107
405-232-5061
Open every weekend,
this market has hundreds of booths indoors
and out.

Oregon

"America's Largest" Antique and Collectible Sale
Portland Expo Center
Exit 306B off Interstate 5
Portland, OR 97232
503-282-0877
As many as 1,300 dealers sell antiques and
collectibles at this
March, July, and
October show. An additional show is held in
November at the
Oregon Convention
Center.

Stars Antique Mall
7027 Southeast
Milwaukee Avenue
Portland, OR 87202
503-239-0346
Antique mall houses
eclectic merchandise
and collectibles.

Pennsylvania

Antique Complex of Fleetwood
Route 222
Fleetwood, PA 19522
619-944-0707
www.antiquecomplex.com
Large shop sells an
eclectic mix of
antiques. There is also
a flea market held on
weekends, April
through October.

Judy Naftulin
7044 Ferry Road
New Hope, PA 18938
215-297-0702
Shop sells European
and American furniture,
lighting, architectural
elements, garden ornaments, mirrors, frames,
and textiles.

Renningers Antique Market
1 mile north of Exit 21 on
   Route 272
Adamstown, PA 19501
717-385-0104 or
717-336-2177
Market is open each
Sunday with hundreds
of dealers in antiques
and collectibles.

Renningers Farmers, Antique, and Flea Market
740 Noble Street
Kutztown, PA 19530
717-385-0104 or
717-336-2177
The counterpart to
the Adamstown
Renningers, this market
happens on Saturdays.

Shupp's Grove
PO Box 892
Adamstown, PA 19501
717-484-4115
This outdoor flea market happens every
Sunday, April through
October. Call for details.

Rhode Island

The Cat's Pajamas
37 Parkway Avenure
Cranston, RI 02905
401-751-8440
Sells 20th century
antiques such as
silver jewelry, Russel
Wright pottery, glassware, and linens. By
appointment only.

General Stanton Flea Market
Old Post Road
Charlestown, RI 02813
401-364-8888
April through November,
this Saturday, Sunday,
and Monday holidays
market has a variety of
merchandise.

South Carolina

Low County Flea Market & Collectibles
Gaillard Auditorium
77 Calhoun Street
Charleston, SC 29401
843-849-1949
Antiques, collectibles,
and estate merchandise
are sold on the third
weekend of every month.

Springfield Flea Market
Intersection of Routes 3
   and 4
Springfield, SC 29146
803-258-3192
A wide variety of items
are available every
Saturday and Monday.

Thieves Market
502 Gadsden Street
Columbia, SC 29201
803-254-4997
Forty dealers sell
antique furniture, dinnerware, and other decorative accessories.

South Dakota

Antique & Furniture Mart
1112 West Main Street
Rapid City, SD 57701
605-341-3345
Sells antique oak furniture, collectibles, glassware, and dinnerware.

Gaslight Antiques
13490 Main Street
Rockerville, SD 57702
605-343-9276
Shop sells 1880's-
1950's furniture, glassware, and jewelry.

Tennessee

Antique Merchant's Mall
2015 8th Avenue S
Nashville, TN 37204
615-292-7811
Thirty-five dealers sell
rare books, furniture,
porcelain, china, crystal, and sterling silver.

Cane-ery Antique Mall
2112 8th Avenue S
Nashville, TN 37204
615-269-4780
American primitive and
oak furniture and decorative hardware are
sold. Also offer cane
and basket repair.

Esau's Antique & Collectible Market
Chilohowee Park
   Fairgrounds
Exit 392 on Interstate 40
Knoxville, TN 37950
800-588-ESAU
This antiques-only
market is open on
the third weekend of
every month.

Hunter Kay Woodland Antiques
5180 Firetower Road
Franklin, TN 37064
615-794-6450
Shop offers eclectic
antiques.

Tennessee State Fairgrounds Flea Market
Nashville, TN
615-862-5016
Held the fourth weekend of each month, except for December when held on the third weekend, this flea market has antiques, collectibles, and estate merchandise.

Texas

Carolyn Thompson's Antique Center of Texas
1001 West Loop North
713-688-4211
Antique mall with over 200 dealers.

C.J. Riley & Co.
109 South Tennessee
McKinney, TX 75069
972-562-1896
Antiques, linens, clothing, and candles.

First Monday Trade Days
PO Box 245
Canton, TX 75103
903-567-6556
Held the weekend preceding the first Monday of each month, this flea market has as many as 5,000 vendors.

Gardens
1818 West 35th Street
Austin, TX 78703
512-451-5490
Along with gardening plants and supplies, this shop sells a variety of accessories.

Liberty & Sons Antiques Market
1506 Market Center Boulevard
Dallas, TX 75207
214-748-3329
Antiques market offers 10,000 square feet of treasures.

Lovers Lane Antique Market
5001 West Lovers Lane
Dallas, TX 75209
214-351-5656
Thirty different antique shops.

The McAllister Collection
101 North Kentucky Street
McKinney, TX 75069
972-562-9497
Architectural elements, antiques, and home accessories.

The Mews
1708 Market Center Boulevard at Oak Lawn
Dallas, TX 75207
214-748-9070
Antique co-op sells all types of high-end French, Continental, and English antiques.

Park Cities Antiques
4908 West Lovers Lane
Dallas, TX 75209
214-350-5893
Miscellaneous antiques.

Room Service by Ann Fox
4354 Lover's Lane
Dallas, TX 75225
214-369-7666
Shop sells antique beds, new and vintage linens, fabrics, paintings, memorabilia.

Emma Lee Turney's Round Top Antiques Fair
PO Box 821289
Houston, TX 77282
281-493-5501
For the first weekends of April and and October, three locations in Round Top, Texas are filled with the best of country antiques.

Shabby Slips
2304 Bissonnet
Houston, TX 77005
713-630-0066
Aged painted furniture, custom slipcovers, architectural elements.

Tesoros Trading Company
209 Congress Avenure
Austin, TX 78701
512-479-8377
Shop sells folk arts and crafts from Peru, Mexico, Gautemala, Brazil, and Germany.

Uncommon Market
2701 Fairmount
Dallas, TX 75201
214-871-2775
Antiques and fixtures.

Uncommon Objects
1512 South Congress Avenue
Austin, TX 78704
512-442-4000
Folky and funky collectibles.

Utah

Antique Collectors' Fair
Salt Palace Convention Center
150 South West Temple
Salt Lake City, UT 84151
801-532-3401
For one weekend each in February, April, June, August, and October, dealers sell antique kitchenware, tools, cowboy items, primitives.

Salt Lake Antiques
279 East 300 S
Salt Lake City, UT 84111
801-322-1273
Shop sells early English and American antiques, silver, paintings, and European furniture.

Vermont

The Store
Route 100
Waitsfield, VT 05673
802-496-4465
Shop sells antiques and collectibles.

Sylvan Hill Antiques
Sylvan Road
Grafton, VT 05146
802-875-3954
Shop sells 17th- and 18th-century English country furniture. By appointment only.

Virginia

Baron's Antiques and Collectibles
1706 East Main Street
Richmond, VA 23223
804-643-0001
Shop sells eclectic antiques.

The Big Flea Market at the Richmond State Fairgrounds
Strawberry Hill, 600 East Laburnum Avenue
Richmond, VA 23222
757-431-9500
Hundreds of dealers sell primarily antiques and collectibles at this monthly flea market.

Copeland House Antiques
20 Main Street
Round Hill, VA 20141
540-338-3453
Shop sells painted furniture and accessories and folk art.

The DC Big Flea Market
Capital Expo Center
4320 Chantilly Place Center
Chantilly, VA 22022
Antiques and collectibles are sold four times a year at this flea market outside Washington, D.C.

Lane Sanson
3423 West Cary Street
Richmond, VA 23221
804-358-0053
Shop sells new accessories and gifts.

**Silverbrooke
Farm Antiques**
15286 Woodgrove Road
Purcellville, VA 20132
540-668-6520
Shop sells decorative architectural pieces and antiques.

**Stuckey's Antique
Emporium**
315 West Broad Street
Richmond, VA 23220
804-320-8299
Sells miscellaneous antiques.

West End Antiques
6504 Horsepen Road
Richmond, VA 23226
804-285-1916
Over 100 dealers sell eclectic antiques, primitives, glassware, wicker.

Washington

**Ruby Montana's
Pinto Pony, Ltd.**
1623 Second Avenue
Seattle, WA 98101
206-443-9363
Shop sells 1950's accessories, 1930's-1960's furniture, and Western nostalgia.

Star Center Mall
829 Second Street
Snohomish, WA 98290
360-568-2131
Around 175 dealers sell a variety of antiques on five different levels.

West Virginia

**A Penny Earned
Antique Mall**
230 Main Street
Weston, WV 26452
304-269-4200

Close to 40 dealers sell a variety of antiques including primitive furniture.

Smokey J Antics
6 Bank Street
Nitro, WV 25243
304-755-9591
Shop sells old toys, trunks, rocking chairs, and clocks.

Spilt Rail Antiques
2580 Benson Drive
Charleston, WV 25302
304-342-6084
Shop sells country antiques and early sporting items. By appointment only.

Wisconsin

**Antiques Mall
of Madison**
4748 Cottage
Grove Road
Madison, WI 53716
608-222-2049
Dealers sell eclectic antiques.

Broadway Antique Mall
115 East Broadway
Monona, WI 53716
608-222-2241
Seventy dealers display at this antique mall.

Larry's Used Furniture
2898 South Syene Road
Madison, WI 53711
608-271-8162
Shop sells salvage doors and windows, furniture, and rugs.

Rummage-O-Rama
Wisconsin State
Fair Park
Milwaukee, WI
414-521-2111
Hundreds of dealers gather one weekend a month for this market of just about everything. Call for dates.

Wyoming

**Old West Antiques and
Cowboy Collectibles**
1215 Sheridan Avenue
Cody, WY 82414
307-587-9014
Shop sells western antiques and collectibles.

**Tomorrow's
Treasures Antiques**
903 East Lincolnway
Cheyenne, WY 82001
307-634-1900
Antiques, glassware, china, and jewelry.

Resources for New Home Furnishings

Anthropologie
One Margaret Way
Ridgely, MD 21685
800-309-2500
www.anthropologie.com
Retail stores across the country sell clothing and electic home furnishings. Catalog.

Banana Republic
5900 North
Meadows Drive
Grove City, OH 43123
800-906-2800
Some branches of this primarily clothing store sell contemporary home furnishings. Catalog.

Crate & Barrel
PO Box 9059
Wheeling, IL 60090
800-323-5461
Branches across the country sell simple and attractive decorative housewares. Catalog.

IKEA
Ikea Catalog Department
185 Discovery Drive
Colmar, PA 18915
800-434-4532
Several large stores sell Swedish-inspired furniture and decorative accessories. Catalog.

Pier 1
PO Box 962030
Fort Worth, TX
  76161-0020
800-447-4371
Branches across the country offer tableware, baskets, wicker furniture, and accessories.

Pottery Barn
PO Box 7044
San Francisco, CA 94133
800-922-5507
Branches across the country offer dinnerware, linens, lamps, furniture, and other home accessories. Catalog.

Restoration Hardware
15 Koch Road, Suite J
Corte Madera, CA 94925
888/243-9720
Branches across the country sell decorative hardware and contemporary furniture and accessories. Catalog.

Sundance
3865 W. 2400 South
Salt Lake City, UT 84120
804-442-2770
www.sundance.com
This catalog-only resource carries artisan-made home accessories, jewelry, and Western-style furnishings.

Whispering Pines
43 Ruane Street
Fairfield, CT 06430
800-836-4662
This catalog-only resource offers rustic cabin-style furniture and accessories.

Williams-Sonoma
100 Northpoint Street
San Francisco, CA 94133
800-541-1262
Branches across the country offer kitchen equipment and accessories. Catalog.

index